To a GREAT Rethinker!

All my best

Adam

Praise for *Rethink*

"*Rethink* is a great book that smashes the myths that too often hold women back. Andi Simon not only skillfully shares the stories of women who have successfully created their own 'blue ocean,' but inspires and guides you to do the same in your life too. This book is a gift that helps women see, feel, and think about their own lives through a fresh lens. Get ready to be inspired!"

—**Renée Mauborgne,** New York Times bestselling author of *Blue Ocean Shift* and *Blue Ocean Strategy*, Professor of INSEAD

"We can do anything we put our minds to, and the stories featured in Andi Simon's *Rethink* are proof of this. I recommend this book to any woman looking for role models or inspiration for success. Keep planning, learning, and working towards your goals. Continue being unapologetically ambitious."

—**Shellye Archambeau,** board director, advisor, and author of *Unapologetically Ambitious*

"*Rethink* is a testament to what women CAN do! This book is a no-nonsense, myth-debunking gem that uses the power of real stories and facts to demonstrate women's true power and potential across multiple industries and roles. Andi's authenticity shines through as she also shares her own journey as a 'myth-smasher' and shows us that success isn't linear and that we don't have to fit in a box. This is a must-read for women looking for a dose of inspiration in their own trailblazing journey."

—**Jessie Medina,** CEO of FEMX Quarters, social entrepreneur, intersectionality consultant, speaker

"Andi Simon's *Rethink* provides powerful examples of how women in the workplace lead to organizational success and creative advancements. These strong leaders who happen to be women took their lives into their own hands and are changing our world as we know it. Sharing stories like these is critical in showcasing models for success, and I hope this book engenders more to come."

—**Cheryl Contee,** CEO of Do Big Things, author of *Mechanical Bull: How You Can Achieve Startup Success*

"With surgical precision, *Rethink* disembowels pernicious myths that propped up the glass ceiling. *Rethink* is not just stories of visionary female leaders, and it is more than a systematic study of their leadership styles or a deconstruction of their successes. *Rethink* is a powerful narrative for a new culture."

—**Max Teplitski,** PhD, Chief Science Officer, Produce Marketing Association

"Dr. Andi Simon's groundbreaking book *Rethink* is a MUST-read! By presenting eleven incredible women's inspiring stories, the author smashes the myths of women in business. Every leader, regardless of industry, needs to read this book! If you're a woman seeking a path in the business world, this is THE book to read, absorb, and then put into practice. Insightfully written, boundary breaking, a sure bestseller!"

—**Elia Gourgouris PhD,** Founder of The Happiness Center

"*Rethink* by Dr. Andi Simon is proof positive that when women are strong, bold, and gutsy, they succeed. Each story serves as a great reminder to keep pushing for equality and prosperity in whatever we choose to do. I recommend this for any professional woman looking to break the glass ceiling in their field."

—**Pat Obuchowski,** MBA, PCC, CEO of inVisionaria, bestselling and award-winning author

"Andi Simon has done a magnificent job with *Rethink* and yes, 'smashing the myths of women in business.' *Rethink* turns myths into reality with marvelous storytelling of women boldly leading the way forward in different industries with the support of other women. Andi points out that we are still a long way from parity and pay parity, and at the Women Business Collaborative (WBC), we know that Power and Parity go together. We know that women and women of color can change the face of the economy and support one another in a new sisterhood. Women lead differently with new leadership from the head, heart, and soul."

—**Edie Fraser,** CEO of Women Business Collaborative (WBC)

"Regardless of where you are in your life's journey, Andi's latest masterpiece gives you the inspiration to 'Rethink' how far you can go. She shares the myth-busting real life stories of successful women who, despite the odds against them, have reached the pinnacle of personal and professional success. Their individual journeys did not always take the path expected, but each one shows how they were able to overcome challenges and conquer obstacles life threw their way. The stories capture your attention and leave you inspired to reach for the stars in your own life. If that isn't enough, Andi ends the book with a how-to guide, giving the thought-provoking tools we can all use to smash myths, get rid of our head trash, and create new successes in our lives. Thank you, Andi Simon, for the gift of *Rethink.* I can now 'Rethink' my own destiny."

—**Robin Stanaland,** Vistage Master Chair

"Andi Simon is a corporate anthropologist—observing the individual stories in a society and interpreting how they come together to shape a culture is her expertise. She uses this unique skill set to explain the bigger picture behind the stories of the incredible women she highlights in her latest book, *Rethink*, and describes how the myths of the past are being shattered by the career trajectories of these trailblazing women. Data-driven analysis is embedded in each riveting chapter about women who are changing the future of business and our entire culture. *Rethink* is a powerful lens through which we can see what is yet to come."

—**Nicole Hittner,** Private Equity/M&A Partner, Ballard Spahr LLP

"*Rethink* by Andi Simon provides an insider view into the myths that plague women's experiences as leaders, regardless of the industry. She masterfully tells these women's stories, both their triumphs and disappointments, illustrating the resiliency and power these women possess. One of the most important contributions of this book is that these women's stories are rooted in their passions, their joys, and their personal goals for fulfillment and contribution. These women are driven, and we are all better as a result. Now, we just need to get out of their way. I look forward to requiring this book in my undergraduate courses that explore issues of leadership, gender, and business."

—**Vicki L. Baker,** MBA, MS, PhD, Professor
of Economics & Management at Albion College, author of
Charting Your Path to Full: A Guide for Women Associate Professors

"Ms. Simon presents a hypothesis that women are smashing career myths by presenting 11 inspiring stories of women who have 'made it' in their chosen fields. She draws on her own experience as well as her anthropology education to try to convince the reader that these myths are entrenched and require us to boldly work to overcome them. Part pep talk, part treatise, the book provides an interesting perspective."

—**Gwen Anson,** Technical Manager, Shell (retired)

"Story is a powerful influence on our species. And so it is that the narratives we tell, and tell ourselves, genuinely come to weave into what we believe is possible. In addressing some of the most profound issues of our time around social inequality, we must consider both the structural constraints put upon us and the cognitive obstacles we place upon ourselves. By bringing attention to individuals who navigated societal barriers through, in part, different ways of thinking about themselves and the worlds they inhabit, Dr. Simon's book brings an essential angle to this critical conversation. Using her anthropologist sensibilities, Andi highlights how a revolutionary smashing of barriers can sometimes come out of pragmatic exploration. By expertly linking together these stories and highlighting their common features, Andi leaves her readers with both motivation and a set of tools to move differently through their world. Dr. Simon's book helped me see the stories I tell myself with fresh eyes. In doing so, she helped me start to dismantle the barriers I construct for the women in my life. Highly recommended!"

—**Peter Boumgarden,** Professor of Practice, Strategy and Organizations, Faculty Director of the Center for Experiential Learning, Washington University in St. Louis, Olin Business School

"In this volume, Andi Simon writes unabashedly and unapologetically for women—drawing attention to their resilience, triumphs, obstacles, and brilliance in their professional lives while simultaneously noting the enmeshed cultural myths that too often constrain and limit. The delight in the individual stories is made richer through Simon's analytic observation about stories more generally: Stories are carriers of cultural ideas that all too often preserve the status quo but also offer the possibility to upend it. When we attend to what is being shared and affirmed in stories we tell about ourselves, as anthropologist Simon does, we can contest and alter. The lives of the women recounted in this volume, eloquently told, offer us new ways to tell stories about ourselves."

—**Rita Denny, PhD,** Executive Director of EPIC

"What a delightful book to read, especially in these times. It's so easy to dwell on what is missing in our society; *Rethink*, on the other hand, tells an optimistic story of addition. The author takes us on an anthropologist's journey of stories, stories of women who have smashed myths, made a difference, and inspire us to do the same."

—**Elisa K Spain,** Leadership Coach and Peer Advisory Board Chair

"Who better than a corporate anthropologist to capture the changing societal and cultural norms that have kept women in the shadows and limited their opportunities to be at the head of the table? Story after story, Andi Simon provides clear evidence and examples of pioneering women breaking down barriers and busting myths that have stood for years as relics of a 'normal' that no longer exists. It is time to set the gender biases aside, acknowledge what is in front of us, and *Rethink* our outdated myths about what women are capable of accomplishing."

—**Konstantinos Apostolopoulos,** co-author of *7 Keys to Navigating a Crisis: A Practical Guide to Emotionally Dealing with Pandemics & Other Disasters*

Rethink

Rethink

SMASHING THE MYTHS OF
WOMEN IN BUSINESS

ANDI SIMON, PhD

FAST
COMPANY
Press

Fast Company Press
New York, New York
www.fastcompanypress.com

This work is being published under the Fast Company Press imprint by an exclusive arrangement with *Fast Company*. *Fast Company* and the *Fast Company* logo are registered trademarks of Mansueto Ventures, LLC. The Fast Company Press logo is a wholly owned trademark of Mansueto Ventures, LLC.

Distributed by Greenleaf Book Group

For ordering information or special discounts for bulk purchases, please contact Greenleaf Book Group at PO Box 91869, Austin, TX 78709, 512.891.6100.

Design and composition by Greenleaf Book Group
Cover design by Greenleaf Book Group and Kimberly Lance
Cover image: ISpiyaphong / iStock / Getty Images Plus

Publisher's Cataloging-in-Publication data is available.

Print ISBN: 978-1-7343248-8-4

eBook ISBN: 978-1-7343248-9-1

Part of the Tree Neutral® program, which offsets the number of trees consumed in the production and printing of this book by taking proactive steps, such as planting trees in direct proportion to the number of trees used: www.treeneutral.com

Printed in the United States of America on acid-free paper

19 20 21 22 23 24   10 9 8 7 6 5 4 3 2 1

First Edition

Rethink is dedicated to all the women
smashing those myths holding them back—
and to my husband, Andy,
who always pushed me forward.

"What you can do, or dream you can, begin it;
boldness has genius, power, and magic in it."

—JOHANN WOLFGANG VON GOETHE

Contents

Foreword

Having spent time with Andi and her husband, Andy, through their Simon Initiative for Entrepreneurship at the Skandalaris Center at Washington University in St. Louis, I know we share a common love for supporting young, aspiring women entrepreneurs. We also share a deep affection and involvement in Washington University. Andi and Andy created the Simon Initiative to help other entrepreneurs, like themselves, find their way from thinking about a big idea to making it happen.

I knew that feeling so well, as a woman who had an idea and turned it into Build-A-Bear Workshop™. It is never easy to think about something and then make it happen. Neither is it easy to create teams of people believing in you and supporting you along the way. Build-A-Bear transformed the way in which children, their parents, and their grandparents experienced retail stores. We were amazed how the children and others could *rethink* what was possible. That kids could fall in love with a bear that they chose, created, dressed, and loved seemed impossible, until it was obvious. That is the theme song of all people changing the world around them. You hear "impossible" a dozen times, and then you do it. Everyone thinks it was just "obvious." It isn't and never will be. Change is so challenging. What we learned was that the experiences of Build-A-Bear Workshop helped us and others see retail through a fresh lens. It was as much about how children *built* their loving companion bear as it was about having a stuffed bear at home.

This is why I found *Rethink: Smashing the Myths of Women in Business* such a timely, awesome book. *Rethink* was designed to tell the stories of women who could be role models for other women who aspire to leap over those proverbial walls and slash through resistant glass ceilings. The book shares the life stories of eleven women, including Andi, as it smashes the myths that could have kept each of these women from ever achieving their successes. As you will see, each story is about a successful woman who did it "her way," much as I have lived my own life. As you read their stories and understand the power of myths, you will realize how these women went charging right through and how our culture and society, business, and home life are being transformed. There is a sea change taking place, and women like these are leading the way for others, both women and men, to follow.

To illustrate, you will listen to a leader in the aerospace field, where there are few women, tell you how she created an exceptional company supporting the aerospace industry. You will learn about how a woman attorney is helping others change the workplace environment so women can become equal partners with equal pay in the legal space. And read carefully to see how other women entrepreneurs took their ideas and turned them into brilliant new companies. Then there is one woman who is turning around companies as their CEO and another who is helping women change how they manage their money. Clever, creative women showing us what can be done if only we ignore the myths holding us back while changing those myths for the future.

What you will also find is that each story helps to change your own mind about what is possible for yourself and other women all around you. You aren't reading about one other woman. You are reading about you and all the other women. At the end, Andi gives you a method for stepping back to see your own life clearly and to rethink what you want to achieve and how you can do it. Don't let the naysayers hold you back. Don't look at what people say is not possible because "women can't." These women could and did. And they—and Andi—want you to do so as well.

As we each look forward to what is to come, we need to create better, more collaborative relationships together so we can build better communities. Women can rise higher, helping us get to a better place for each of us. Andi wants us to "rethink" who we are and what we can do, and then go do it!

It is special to be sharing with you this book, and Andi and I both hope you share your stories with us so we can help other women see what they can do, just like you have done.

Maxine K. Clark | CEO, Clark-Fox Family Foundation
Founder, Build-A-Bear Workshop
INspirator, The Delmar DivINe
Managing Partner, Prosper Women's Capital
Executive in Residence, Washington University in
St. Louis—John M. Olin School of Business

PART ONE

The Reason for This Book

Introduction

This book emerged from the success of my first book, *On the Brink: A Fresh Lens to Take Your Business to New Heights*. *On the Brink* won an Axiom 2017 Bronze Best Business Book Award. The book sold well and brought in many great clients. However, much to my chagrin, as I reviewed what I had written, I realized that all but one of the case studies were about men—CEOs of companies that had stalled or gotten stuck, and my company had to help them start growing again.

My publisher, Tanya Hall, CEO of Greenleaf Book Group, is a successful businesswoman and writer in her own right. I asked her: "How did I, or we, do that?" We both laughed a bit and realized it was time to write the next book. This book was going to be about women and what I saw happening all around me. These women were literally smashing the myths of women in business, defying everything they were told about women in business. They were boldly leading the way forward in their industries, and their stories needed to be told. I soon realized that a new mythology was emerging, and these women were the ones who could frame it, live it, and change the way our society thought about women and their growing force in the world of business and society.

Today, women are driving a coevolution of previously unseen size and scope. Women are challenging long-held beliefs about what they can and cannot do. Despite the theories of evolutionary psychologists and others that women evolved to stay in the home to care for children so men could hunt, farm, trade, go to war, and protect their homes, these women are breaking out of these genetic determinants and showing how they can do everything men can do, albeit differently, and in some cases better. These myths are being rewritten by women who have capitalized on education, the demands of the marketplace, and new possibilities that have emerged. Reluctantly, men are realizing they don't have all the solutions to societal or business problems, thereby creating an opening for women to rethink these long-held beliefs as they establish a new norm and lead the way forward for others.

Beyond *Lean In*

When I began to write this book, people asked me if I wanted to write about Sheryl Sandberg or Meg Whitman, or perhaps Mary Barra or Indra Nooyi, all well-known and highly successful women who have led major firms and helped develop vast wealth. They are, indeed, highly successful women in their own right. Their stories can and do inspire other women to want to achieve significant roles in large corporations, with the associated prestige and wealth that comes with it. But something else was taking place as women were moving into all levels of industry and business, and that was the story I wanted to share.

While some women have become billionaires, they are still a mini-minority. There were only 319 women billionaires in 2018. That was an impressive increase, since back in 2015, there were only 187. There is some progress at the top. However, that increase is less impressive when you realize that 2,433 men were also billionaires in 2018. While much more remains to be done, these women set a standard for others to reach for and a style to emulate.

The funnel, however, is not filling up as fast as we might like. Sheryl Sandberg's *Lean In* was a push to increase the number of women in CEO roles in S&P 500 companies. In 2017, the momentum she was championing came to a hard stop. Only 5.4 percent of CEOs in S&P 500 firms were women. Despite Sheryl Sandberg's urging women to "Lean In," companies have not been opening up and moving women into leadership and senior management positions. As evident in LeanIn.org's 2018 research conducted with McKinsey, the advancement of women in the large corporate workplace was not moving. As they wrote, "Progress isn't just slow—it's stalled."

The largest companies did not seem to be moving in the right direction to open the gates to women. In fact, many of the women who were on the brink of moving into those senior C-suite positions jumped off the ladder because the obstacles were overwhelming, and the road was filled with men who seemed to be deliberately trying to stop their progress. As Susan Chiara wrote in 2017, "The impact of gender is hard to pin down decisively. But after years of biting their tongues, believing their ranks would swell if they simply worked hard, many senior women in business are concluding that the barriers are more deeply rooted and persistent than they wanted to believe."

These myths about women are being manipulated to keep them out of leadership roles. Women are seen as dependable rather than visionary. They also tend to be uncomfortable with self-promotion and are more likely to be criticized when they do grab the spotlight. Men remain threatened by assertive women. Most women are not socialized to be unapologetically competitive. Those who thought they were on their way to somewhere important get discouraged. They begin to wonder what they are really trying to do—and why it is so hard to find purpose and meaning in the positions they thought were important to pursue.

It turns out the problem is far deeper than simply those women trying to enter the C-suite. Attorneys are finding that men often forget that female attorneys are their colleagues and think of them more as support staff, asking them to clean their plates or get their coffee. Women dentists complain they still get men telling them they are taking a spot in dental school that a man should have. And women in number two positions are being asked to be the back ups to the C-suite men, not their equals.

And, of course, there is that pay gap. Women still do not earn as much as men, and that wage gap remains a major challenge. In 2000, women earned 73 cents for every dollar a man earned. By 2016, the gender pay gap had shrunk to 80 cents to the dollar, which is an improvement, but we have a ways to go still.

There is another way of looking at the situation women are facing. While substantial progress has been made, something profound is taking place as women are moving into these jobs, and they are beginning to change the myths and norms that have kept them out. Perhaps *Lean In* wasn't focused on the right companies. Maybe women are moving forward, taking on significant roles in smaller or middle-market companies, or starting their own businesses, entering and reaching parity in a wide array of fields and growing in numbers among all the professions. Perhaps they are succeeding to push through the proverbial glass ceiling, opening doors to power and profits, but in different ways.

What is success anyway? This is an important question to ask, particularly when women, me included, have had to leap over those walls that society keeps throwing up to keep us in "our place"—be it the home, kitchen, or nursery—and out of the C-suite or the boardroom.

As I stop to see what is happening through a fresh lens, I notice that something is taking place under the LeanIn.org radar. I have been watching it in the work I do and the women leaders I support. I see a little of it in the speaking engagements for CEOs that I have done. While most of the CEOs in the room are men, a few more women appear in each group each time I attend. Women are beginning to inherit family firms, start innovative new companies, and push through some of the barriers.

We were all excited to see the election of a record number of women into Congress, the expanded role of women in local and state government, and the power of the women's soccer team successes in capturing the world's attention. Even if they had to sue for equal compensation to that which men were getting, the worldwide excitement over the women's soccer team became rightfully important.

These emerging women may not be moving into the largest of the firms, and they may not yet be the CEOs or the billionaires, but they are moving into areas that men did not believe women could perform in and where they were not wanted. Those industries still exist, from the executive and directorial levels of Hollywood to aerospace, where there are few women. The talented women are starting to emerge, but the walls are tall and the ceilings difficult to break through.

But their time is coming. What I am seeing is the rising place of women. As John Seely Brown once wrote, "The way forward is all around us, if only we can see it." There is no single factor here. Instead, a convergence of forces are coming together to provide opportunities for women, and they are capitalizing on them. From their majority numbers in higher education, to those entrepreneurs opening and running their own businesses, to the rise of female support networks, women are taking advantage of the possibilities, finding the gaps, and seizing the moment.

The women in this book are redefining what our society believes to be "true" and in the process are challenging the walls that keep women in, the glass ceilings they have tried to break through, and the world as men and even women have long thought it was "supposed to be." What is so exciting is to see the size and scope of these changes across a wide range of industries by so many talented women. Whether it is #MeToo or the sheer weight of women leading industry and culture, those walls are falling, faster and faster.

This doesn't mean that men are not still putting up barriers and barricades. As Kim Elsesser wrote in 2018 in her Forbes.com article "Female Lawyers Face Widespread Gender Bias," women attorneys continue being stereotyped as women, not as accomplished lawyers.

This includes everything from being mistaken for janitors, administrators, or court personnel to having men ask them to clean their plates. A woman attorney shared, "I have frequently been assumed to be a court reporter. In my own firm, I've been asked if I am a legal administrative assistant on multiple occasions, even after making partner." The biases are profound, and changing them is a persistent problem everywhere.

Smashing Myths

While interviewing these women and many others, I realized how they were changing me and my own story. I was getting pulled into their stories and was personally affected as a result. Stories change us as we listen to them, read them, or watch them. We become a part of the story. We get engaged with the storyteller. While I knew that intellectually, it wasn't until I did the interviews that I began to see how my whole idea about the book was changing, and the women who were sharing their stories were, in fact, changing me.

Did these women know they were "smashing the myths" at the time? Not really. Most of them were realists, understanding that there were always going to be hurdles to leap over. In some ways they were simply pushing forward, and in the process they achieved results that amazed even them. They were in the labyrinth that Alice H. Eagly and Linda L. Carli write about in their book *Through the Labyrinth: The Truth About How Women Become Leaders*. As stated in the book, there is no single path to follow. It is a maze of twists and turns to tackle. And in the stories these women share, you will see how they defied the myths and created a new story where women are pushing down walls, breaking through glass ceilings, and launching new societal norms that are opening up and allowing their greatness to come through.

The women interviewed in this book are not alone or unique. As you read their stories, you will see how they are pushing through in innovative ways and smashing the following cultural myths they encountered along the way:

Myth 1: Women Can't Be Great Entrepreneurs
Myth 2: Women Are Not Good Leaders
Myth 3: Women Cannot Run a Fashion Business
Myth 4: Women Shouldn't Be Lawyers
Myth 5: Women Cannot Manage Money
Myth 6: Women Do Not Make Good College Presidents
Myth 7: Women Can't Be Geoscientists
Myth 8: Women Aren't Fit for Careers in Aerospace
Myth 9: Women Cannot Rise to Upper Management Roles
Myth 10: Women Don't Belong in IT
Myth 11: Anthropologists Don't Work in Business

As you take this journey, you will meet Jamie Candee, who has been leading others since she was in high school, when she first began helping people become their best selves. Celeste Ford will share how she created an award-winning company to help the aerospace industry develop high-tech solutions in highly innovative, impactful ways. You will also meet Stephanie Breedlove, a highly successful entrepreneur who had to disregard her parents when they didn't think she and her husband could build a successful business. And then there's Delora Tyler, who learned that as an African American woman, if she wanted to be heard in the workplace and have her ideas appreciated, she would need to start her own company. Today she can take any company from 0 to 60, despite all obstacles put in front of her. You will also meet Evelyn Medvin, a highly renowned geologist, who will tell you how she bucked all the resistors who never thought a woman could cut it in the field and uses her ability to "see" geology to find oil where others can't. Maria Gallo will discuss how she turned a struggling university into a thriving institution. Babette Ballinger overcame all types of obstacles to create and grow a successful manufacturing business in the fashion industry. Andrea Kramer will tell you how she defied what others told her and became a successful attorney. Janine Firpo will relay how she helps women manage and grow their earnings and savings. You will also meet Sam Radocchia, who will show you how she is crushing it in the IT industry. And then there's me, an anthropologist who found the perfect partnership in business and anthropology to help companies see themselves through a fresh lens and course-correct their way to success.

The Myths That Frame Your Own Story

Each of these women tell you their stories so you can rewrite your own, even better. As you read their stories, I invite you to ask yourself how your beliefs, and those of others around you—from family to friends to media and to teachers—have kept you thinking about what you can't do as opposed to what is right there waiting for you to accomplish.

Before you get discouraged, I want you to know that each of these women faced the same or similar challenges and continue to do so today. Yet they are smashing the myths before them, and they want you to do so as well.

When people share their stories, they do so to give their wisdom. When this happens, we can activate our own story and change it. Each story shared in this book is the gift of each woman to help us see, feel, and think about our own lives through a fresh lens. The stories are also framing a new mythical reality where women are not who society once thought they were. Some of these women, at times, were slaying a metaphorical dragon. Others went from rags to riches. Several were on a quest. Typically, they were on a journey, often without a clear destination, with many hurdles to overcome, challenges to conquer, and rewards to amass. Their stories are as much about becoming who they wanted to be as they are about profits and success.

I hope their stories will help you see a pathway for you and others like you. It cannot be done alone. Women need others to learn from, model themselves after, and share their common stories. They need a culture that supports their achievements and helps them overcome the challenges. These women are part of this new community, one that you can also be a part of.

As you read these stories, think about yourself and where you are in your own life's journey. Think about what you would like to create and how it feels to be where you are right now. Are you letting your heart lead you? Or is your brain hijacking your journey? Let go, if you can, of whatever it is that is keeping you back, and follow these women, one story at a time. As you do, think about the stories that have become the mythology you believe to be true. And know that you, too, can smash them to become the woman you know you are and can be.

After each story, you will find my thoughts as an anthropologist in the From the Observation Deck section. Anthropology is grounded in the assumption that people often don't know what they are doing or why they are doing it. Only by observing them go through their stories and experiencing their journeys with them can we capture what we see happening. I call this From the Observation Deck so that I can pause at the end of each chapter with you and share some thoughts and insights that might help you better understand what we covered. I will also share how anthropology can help you break through the barriers you are currently facing as you challenge the myths, so you can craft your own story.

At the end of this book I have provided a tool kit and directory of resources, networking organizations, and women who are helping women get their businesses started and thrive. I created this section so you wouldn't have to do it alone. Here you will find a community of additional storytellers in the ready, waiting to help.

How Our Myths and Stories
Shape Who We Are

"To be a person is to have a story to tell."

—*Isak Dinesen (Karen Blixen),*
author of Out of Africa

Imagine you were out in the savannah seventy-five thousand years ago. The men have had an arduous day hunting gazelles and remarkably caught one for the camp to cook for dinner. The women have provided the family's meal, collecting the roots and tubers, fruits, and berries. Game hunting was unpredictable. Without the women's foraging, the camp might not have ever survived waiting for the guys to catch their game. But on this day the men outran the gazelle and brought it back for their family, clan, or tribe to share.

What does everyone do that evening? Sit around the campfire, sharing the stories about the day's hunting, where the game was found, how they shot it with their arrows, and how they followed it after it was hit. The more experienced hunters might use the day as a way to educate those younger men. Together they sang songs and spoke about what they had learned and how their skills had improved. The men were always the heroes in their stories, and their journeys were always filled with challenges and failures. The gods might have helped. They may have even thanked the gazelle.

The stories they created and shared may have dramatized their successes while downplaying their difficulties. In the process of telling their stories, they created great myths. In their mythology, the men put into place the way they wanted women, children, the elders, and themselves to see their world and to live in it. They often tied their human lives with those of the gods, the animals, and the earth. It was one world, in a sense, and their myths and stories helped them understand and protect themselves from the vagaries of life.

The power of humans comes from their ability to create and share stories. You might wonder how stories could be so important on so many different levels. Our evolution has been a coevolution—part genetics and part culture, both leading to natural selection. In Joseph Henrich's book *The Secret of Our Success: How Culture Is Driving Human Evolution, Domesticating Our Species, and Making Us Smarter*, he builds the case for how we have evolved. He states that it has been more than just genetic evolution. Rather, our ability to talk, create a culture and the stories that made it come alive, and share myths that helped keep people together were intrinsic part of our evolution.

Humans have evolved into who we are today in great part because of our time around the campfire sharing stories. Of course, technological innovations, from fire to software, have spurred our transformation. But the most important part of our development was our ability to be great storytellers. That's what makes us human. Unlike other primates, we live in the fictional worlds we create through our ability to imagine realities and make them our own. Humans are herd animals, and we like to be with others like ourselves. And we share our stories to affirm our place in that society.

Equally important is how storytelling enabled us to develop the skills needed to adapt to particular environments. Unlike other creatures that diversified to fit their environments, we remain one species that evolved by using our ability to create, share, and continue to improve upon our cultural and physical tools as well as our collaborative methods for problem-solving.

That is why there is such power in the stories we create and the way we share them. Further, people tell stories that tend to follow a hero who has a challenge to conquer and the journey that has taken him—or her—on their way with metaphorical dragons to conquer, travails to overcome, and somehow a way to overcome the hurdles and rise again, triumphant.

I think you will hear the same heroic stories captured in those shared by the women in this book. As you read about them in the chapters ahead, listen closely to how each one found her mentor or guide and managed to overcome obstacles to finally emerge the hero of her own story.

Why Is an Anthropologist Writing about Businesswomen?

Anthropology captured my imagination and my interests when, as an undergraduate, I discovered the cultural differences in how people created, shared, manipulated, and truly believed their myths and stories about who they were, where they came from, and why they did things. This mythology became an important part of their realities. Their stories captured the very essence of their culture. They were less important as truths than as the way people made sense of their truths.

Years later, I had a career all set out. It was my own personal story. I had my PhD. I was a tenured assistant professor and a published author, and I was running a master lecture series while producing a TV series for CBS on change in America.

It was around that time that I was introduced to a group of Citibankers at a cocktail party with my husband, who was an executive there. They invited me to help them change. And in that instant my future was serendipitously transformed. I spent the next fifteen years in banking and then another seven in healthcare as an executive, helping these organizations change.

Like the companies, I also had to change. I had to change my clothes and put on a suit to fit in. I had to put my PhD in my back pocket. I was now a senior vice president or an executive vice president in a bank, not an anthropologist. I was sitting at meetings with all the men and realizing how I would have to change how I spoke, led, and got things done. Occasionally, I wandered around the house in the middle of the night trying to figure out who I was and what I was really doing.

What I quickly learned was how to play in a new game, if I was going to play to win. I had to learn the mythology. I had to adapt my voice, my storytelling, my conversations with bosses, subordinates, customers, and even my friends to become a different player on a new stage. This anthropologist quickly became a successful businesswoman, a leader doing what others did not know or want to do: change.

The times were changing. Deregulation was changing banking. Managed care was changing healthcare. The prior leaders were good at what always had been the accepted ways of doing things. And they were looking at me to help them change. I made it up to an executive vice president of First National Bank of Highland, a division of M&T Bank, only to discover that glass ceiling. I would go to board meetings with forty-nine men and me. I learned then what it was to be stereotyped into roles that were being created by men for men— and I could either play the role or find another place to play.

The Purpose of Myths

Out of this experience, I became fascinated by the power of myths and stories to keep us in our place in our societies. So many cultures have had essentially the same mythologies. They had different ways of telling those stories, but with recurring themes, all designed to explain the common challenges of human lives. Those myths weren't simply entertainment, Star Trek–style. Instead, they had tremendous power to organize, stabilize, and control people. Myths and cultural traditions are created and sustained over time because they help people make sense out of their experiences, relationships, and those unknowns that seem to challenge personal survival in a world of uncertainties. As humans evolved, myths, cultural rituals, and shared stories essentially explained a phenomenon so people could understand why they did something or why something should be done.

Joseph Campbell's *The Hero with a Thousand Faces* captures how mythology is the underlying foundation in every civilization and underpins each individual's personal consciousness. His discussion of the "monomyth" shows how, regardless of time or place, humans created myths with similar themes, characters, purpose, and format. In ancient times, the myth provided the listener with a truth that could then be interpreted, shared, and modified to fit the group and their own culture. Understanding their realities was up to them, not someone insisting on a certainty that only an authority figure (king, priest, noble) would control.

As Campbell writes: "The psyche, as a reflection of the world and man, is a thing of such infinite complexity that it can be observed and studied from a great many sides. It faces us with the same problem that the world does: because a systematic study of the world is beyond our powers, we have to content ourselves with mere rules of thumb and with aspects that particularly interest us. Everyone makes for himself his own segment of the world and constructs his own private system, often with air-tight compartments, so that after a time it seems to him that he has grasped the meaning and structure of the whole. But the finite will never be able to grasp the infinite."

If our myths become essential for our perceptions of reality but are illusions, not truths, how do we change them when they are no longer working as they might have in the past? To understand this query, we must reflect on what we have learned about how our brains create our realities. The brain takes data or facts and turns them into stories that then become our realities. Those stories are powerful. Once created, our brain sees only what conforms to that story.

Changing the story is hard work. You literally have to start seeing things through a new, fresh lens.

"Research is showing that stories physically change the way the brain is working, and when you're in this changed state, then it's possible to change your life experiences," says Paul J. Zak, PhD, the neuroeconomist whose organization, ZESTx Labs, studies how and why stories engage us and change our brains, usually for the better. Further, neuroscience research is showing us how the brain takes information and uses stories to make sense out of it, regardless of where the person is located or the language in which they are reading the story.

These stories influence how we see our worlds and evaluate what people are doing in them. New data that does not fit our storyline is ignored or deleted, as our brain hijacks new information that doesn't fit what we believe to be true. In other words, we can only see what we believe, and we only believe what we can see.

Breaking Free from the Myths That Control Us

Our myths lend power to the person over the challenges that surround them. Myths explain, empower, stabilize, and elevate meaning in the life of a believer. They put daily life into a broader context and enable society to establish controls and order among disparate people within and beyond the family, the clan, and the tribe, who may not share common personal experiences or goals but who are all living in a similar world. These are fictions, but they play important roles in real lives.

When it comes to the place of women in all societies, evolutionary psychologists argue that humans evolved over millennia by forming an adaptive reality in which they created mythologies and cultural norms that separated men and women. Society placed women in the home, typically securing their roles there as mother, housekeeper, weaver, and keeper of the daily order. Men went to hunt the game, farm the fields, fight the wars, and trade the goods. The mythology served multiple purposes, both establishing the proper roles for people but also enabling the human brains to evolve with the right scripts and roles passing from one generation to the next, adapting along the way but securing society through these cultural truths. The myths could be shared, and in the process of telling each other about them, people ensured that others embraced the norms and followed them.

The evolutionary psychologists' arguments emerged in the mid-1990s when they began to look at gender through a Darwinian lens. Gender differences, they argued, have evolved through sexual selection to the point that they have become the way we are, locked into our genes. David Geary, PhD, posed the foundation of his argument around the different purposes that men and women have in our society. Men are to spread their genes by impregnating as many women as they can, investing their reproductive energies in having offspring. And women are bound by their roles in having those offspring and raising them. Women want a man who is focused on them and on caring for their children. These roles explain how this thinking has led to the cultural values of all societies, with women pushed into the home and men able to have multiple mates and increase their reproductive value for human evolution.

While we might think of men having children with many women today as undesirable, even evil, the Masai in Tanzania or Kenya have ten wives as a symbol of their prestige and power, and with those wives, many children. Evolutionary psychologists suggest that biological evolution has made men and women significantly different in how they select a mate, what they expect each other to do, and where they see themselves and others on a competitive playing field. As they suggest from their research, "Men will continue to be philandering, non-nurturing and sex-focused, and women will continue to be mothering keepers-of-the-hearth."

Research on how girls and boys play tends to support their arguments. For example, in Vivian Paley's work *Boys and Girls: Superheroes in the Doll Corner*, she sets forth her experiments to better understand the psychology of gender. As a teacher, Paley wanted to understand how to make boys behave. In her classrooms, boys were always the agents of chaos. They took over the "block corner" and built forts, battleships, and other engines of war and then went into recurring battle with all the loud sounds associated with men at war. And they loved it.

Whereas the girls kept to the dolls corner, where they and their dolls were dressed up, and they took care of the dolls as if they were their babies. Their conversations were about fictional boyfriends, and they tried to engage one of the boys to become their prince or daddy. More often, they were the "victims" that the boys needed when they were playing pirates or other bad guys. Paley was troubled by the stereotypes that were being lived out in her classroom, year after year, as she taught school.

Paley wrote about how storytelling and fantasy play had an amazing impact on children's academic and social development as they made sense of their worlds, adapted to their classrooms, learned how to communicate with peers and the opposite sex, and got things done together. Most important for our work, she tried hard to get the girls to play with the blocks and not simply turn them over to another kitchen in which to cook, and to get the boys to use the girls' area to learn how to be nurturing. Unfortunately, it never worked. They seemed hardwired to be who they were—strong, tough guys and sweet, adoring girls.

The evolutionary psychologists and the educators were all coming to a conclusion that girls will be girls and boys will be boys, regardless of how hard society tries to balance opportunities for women or redirect the attitudes of men. Their research made us worried that change was impossible. If women have become who they are through evolutionary changes and the way in which cultures defined what women could do, could they break out of their destiny and change their cultures? Was there perhaps another way?

One more side to this research is those who claim our gender roles have much more variation, and that variation comes from our learned culture. Society, they say—and not our genes—determines how we react to our biology.

What becomes particularly testy is that the researchers and their findings seemingly match their own gender, with men advocating evolutionary causation and women defending cultural determinism and its potential for transformation. They argue that the men, who hold high-status positions, are promoting theories that maintain the patriarchal status quo whereas women, some of them self-described feminists, see a science that allows for more change.

If there is a genetic basis for what men and women are supposed to do, can women challenge the environmental psychologists and push past their affection for dolls in order to bust open those myths? As an anthropologist, I have to wonder if there is another way to think about men, women, boys, and girls and how we have gotten to where we are today.

In his book *The Secret of Our Success: How Culture Is Driving Human Evolution, Domesticating Our Species, and Making Us Smarter*, Joseph Henrich states that culture has made us who we are today but can also change what we are becoming for the future. Cultural learning, such as in storytelling, reaches directly into our brains and changes them. These neurological functions are part of how we have been able to become ecologically dominant over other species. Our unique evolutionary advantage, according to environmental psychologists, is not just our ability to process information with "improvisational intelligence." Neither are our brains full of genetically endowed cognitive abilities so that we can solve problems every day, finding the right solutions so we can survive. Nor is our advantage due solely to a third theory that focuses on our sociability and how we cooperate with others.

Instead, Henrich has set forth the research that integrates these theories into one that understands the intersection of nature, nurture, biological evolution, and culture. He states that cultural evolution gave us the information and the ability to discern complex adaptive behaviors that changed over time, and these behaviors can continue to adapt as we respond to new environmental situations. The power of our culture has made us what we are today. And the plasticity of that culture can help us adapt for the future. It has happened before, and it will again.

So if our culture has a certain plasticity, how do we redefine the role of women in our society and change the mythology? If over our history our brains changed to create stories and myths about what women are and how they are supposed to perform in our societies, seemingly those myths can change again. In the chapters ahead, I will introduce you to ten women who will show you how they are rethinking the cultural myths in their respective fields and how they are smashing these myths to break through and challenge our culture and their roles in it. And I will share with you my own story.

From the Observation Deck

As humans, we live our myths in our daily lives. These myths are stories that become our realities. These stories are passed down from one mother to their daughters and sons, from one schoolteacher to their students, from one friend to another, and from one boss to their employees. Men and women don't even reflect on whether these myths are true. They simply become what is real.

In turn, we create our stories from them. These stories become our perceptions of reality, guiding our lives with others. We share them, as we have always done over time. Myths help societies sustain their core values and build their belief systems, helping to control people and their behaviors so they can live together. For humans, myths have immense importance with a larger social purpose.

If you believe something to be true, challenges to those truths are easily discarded, even when you know something is wrong with the myth and how it reflects your own reality. As I worked through the stories these women were sharing, I realized they were challenging—indeed "smashing"—those myths and soaring way above what people had always thought was impossible. Those women who were breaking through the barriers were doing so in creative ways and setting new rules for the games they were playing. It was worthwhile to pause and, in an anthropological way, take a fresh look at what they were doing. During our conversations, I marveled at how their stories were becoming realities and how their new successes could begin to change what others believed to be truths.

The stories in this book, while inspiring on an individual level, also tell us about what is happening beyond the lives of these unique individuals. The anthropologist Mary Catherine Bateson reminds us that we are all storytellers. Our stories reflect our shifting lives. Through our stories we make sense of those twists and turns. They allow us to make meaningful, organized, coherent lives. They also show us something important about what is emerging in our society and transforming our culture.

Many of the women I interviewed spoke about how they were raised and what they were taught or able to do as they were growing up. They come from quite different backgrounds, but the recurring theme is that they were raised in good homes with hardworking parents who wanted them to get a good education.

These women knew no limits and feared the few that were there. Each of the women I interviewed, and many more whom I met and spoke with, could see the possibilities to become who they are today. They simply needed a way to do it so they could fulfill their own personal promise to themselves.

All of these stories are going to show you how each woman was able to find her way and escape from the socially accepted norms while keeping her personal identity, professional strength, and desire to achieve something that truly mattered to her and to others.

These women chose to share their stories because their experiences mattered to them and shaped who they are today. Their stories can also become the new standards by which we set the norms for our culture and our society. Rather than believing that women *can't* or *don't* or *shouldn't*, it is time to believe that women *can* and *should* and *will*. Social propriety based on gender is dated and in need of reshaping. The social programming out there is strong and pervasive, and the time is ripe to get out the new message.

Stories that become myths and embrace the new truths are powerful. Once we believe that something is the way it is, we share it with others and look upon outsiders as strangers or deviants. Women need to come together in groups that share similar values, beliefs, and ways of doing things so they can mimic each other, bond, and share their stories. They need a community with a shared culture. With access to such a community and culture, they can receive the support and encouragement they need to rewrite their own stories and create new truths.

The women in this book have created a shared community for you to reference and emulate. It is my hope that you will enjoy the stories and that you will begin to create some of your own as you reach out to join or create your own communities of support. In the chapters ahead, you will see that becoming the heroine you've always aspired to be is possible, and these stories will show you the way. If you happen to find yourself wanting to say thank you to the storytellers in this book, send me a note at info@andisimon.com, and I'll be sure to pass it along.

PART TWO

The Myths and the Women Who Smashed Them

Women Can't Be Great Entrepreneurs

_____

"The future belongs to those who believe
in the beauty of their dreams."

—_Eleanor Roosevelt_

Imagine it is the 1990s. You are finishing up your college education and are ready to head into the workforce. Perhaps you envision a life as a professional and as a wife and mother. You have this dream in your mind that is launching you on your journey. You know you are a smart, energetic woman. When growing up, you did it all, just right. Then you head into your first job at a large firm, only to discover that working in a cubicle isn't part of your dream. You are too isolated in your job. You were expecting to run a business, not a project. And you know your talent is far more exceptional than the bosses seem to acknowledge.

This story is not uncommon among the women I interviewed for this book. Starting out, they were so confident, and then, after a series of setbacks, they felt uncertain. For each of them, their first jobs filled them with anxiety, discomfort, and self-doubt, but then a whole series of societal changes launched them into new places they might never have imagined. By looking inward, they were able to see they weren't the problem. The problem was trying to be themselves in an environment that didn't fit. By turning their ideas into innovations, they were able to build better businesses. However, they didn't start out knowing this or what their particular business was going to become. They weren't even focused on becoming entrepreneurs. They just knew that the corporate environment was not right for them.

This conflict does not necessarily happen to everyone. But it certainly did to Stephanie Breedlove. Somehow, Stephanie was able to take an idea that came out of her challenges and turn it into a successful business that she grew over the course of twenty years. Her company, Breedlove & Associates, emerged out of her own need to pay her nanny's taxes.

In 1992, Breedlove founded her payroll company to make it easier for parents to pay their nannies. It began small, and she self-funded its growth, which averaged 20 percent per year.

By 2012, the business was profitable and had hit $9 million in annual sales. Stephanie's pain led her company to become the experts in the nanny-tax business, serving over ten thousand clients.

One day she got a call from Care.com's CEO, Sheila Marcelo. Sheila was aware of Breedlove & Associates because their companies had a content-sharing relationship. There were real compatibilities between the two companies, and Marcelo offered Breedlove almost $40 million for her company. Stephanie thought her company was worth more and walked away from the offer. We'll tell you what happened after we look at the myth Stephanie was facing as a woman in the 1990s who was starting her own business while raising her family.

The Myth

To understand the magnitude of what Stephanie accomplished, it's important to set her achievements in the social context in which she was living. American Express has been capturing and sharing the US Census Bureau data on women-owned businesses since 2010. Based on their 2012 survey, and projected through 2018, the numbers tell an amazing story about what life was like in the latter part of the twentieth century and what is happening all around us today.

Between 1972 and 2018, the number of women-owned businesses increased thirty-one times, increasing from 402,000 or 4.6 percent of all firms in 1972 to 12.3 million or 40 percent of all firms in 2018. Along with this surge in women-owned businesses, women in the workforce rose from 230,000 to 9.2 million, a forty-fold growth. Revenues in women-owned firms increased from their 1972 levels of $8.1 billion, 0.3 percent of all firms' revenue, to $1.8 trillion, 4.3 percent of total firm revenue in 2018.

It certainly sounds as if the times are a-changing. The historical literature about businesswomen and women in businesses is rich with different perspectives, all trying to better understand the challenges facing women who entered the workforce either as an employee or as an owner of a business. Clearly, women's ventures into business were as much a reflection of the times and the culture in which they were living as it was about their own ingenuity, creativity, and desire to develop a business venture. Stephanie was on the brink of a major transformation in the opportunities for women to start and operate entrepreneurial businesses, and our culture and society had to catch up.

As we look back on the history of this country, we can understand why society needed to catch up with Stephanie. In the seventeenth century, Dutch colonists in New York City believed in a highly matriarchal society where women inherited money and lands and often became business owners. These women benefited from the customs and laws of the Dutch colony and had the freedom to share in the prosperous trading center. The demand for business acumen and innovation enabled women to leverage their education to open their own businesses. Most of these women, and even the men, had no separation between their homes and their work. They were using space in a blended manner, so men and women typically ran their businesses from their homes, allowing women to take care of their families and also be businesswomen.

Nevertheless, as America was settled, women were living in gender-defined cultures where the norms of the times sanctioned women who worked. Many of their businesses were alehouses, brothels, taverns, or retailing, and women were often seamstresses or provided other in-home services. Women were supposed to be frail, not assertive; gentle, not imaginative. Those who were able to develop substantial businesses were successful despite societal norms.

When the British defeated the Dutch and took over New York in 1664, they curtailed the freedom for women to own and run businesses. Under English laws, married women lost a great deal of their freedoms to represent themselves in business or in court. By 1700, women's roles had changed, and the number engaged in business, in services, or in trade declined. There was even a sharp decline in the number of women inheriting real property.

Throughout the nineteenth century, women went into businesses more often out of necessity than from a desire to convert an idea into an enterprise. There was a surge in female entrepreneurs as women gained the right to vote, and their businesses typically served the needs of other women. As the economy expanded in everything from textiles to home appliances, railroads, and personal care products, women began to find ways to create and grow their own businesses.

In the early twentieth century, women continued to launch and grow their own businesses. During the 1930s, women were often struggling to survive, trying to find work where they could sustain their homes and families. During the Second World War, women went into the workforce to replace the men who were serving in the military. Many women also started businesses of their own to fill what they saw as unmet needs. They were creative and used their talents to develop new ways of solving old problems. Pauline Trigere, for instance, came to New York from Paris in 1937 and started a tailoring business for women's clothes that turned into a high-end fashion house. Estée Lauder was introduced to the chemistry used to create products at her uncle's beauty products company. He taught her how to provide "the power to create beauty." After the war she created the Estée Lauder Company. At first the company sold its skin care products to beauty salons and hotels, and then through all types of marketing, from telephone to tell-a-woman, it became the beauty empire we all know today.

Others, like Lillian Vernon, created home-based businesses so they could raise a family while developing a serious business. The myth is all about how she started her business by investing her wedding gift money and filling orders from her kitchen table. Similarly, Mary Crowley founded Home Interiors and Gifts as a way to help women throw home parties and earn a living, avoiding the negativity surrounding working women.

Through the postwar years, two trends were affecting women. While the myth was that the nuclear family of a mother, a father, and children was the best way to live, divorce rates began to rise. Many women found themselves back in the labor force, often as the sole provider for their families. When the recession hit, many women lost their jobs and had to find other ways to survive. Women such as Mary Kay Ash and Ruth Fertel, of Ruth's Chris Steak House, became instrumental in helping women find a pathway during the 1960s and 1970s. Ruth Fertel had a particular purpose in helping women. Divorced and having difficulty finding sufficient work, she mortgaged her home and bought a restaurant, Chris Steak House. She knew nothing about restaurants or steaks. But within six months she had doubled her salary and was attracting local politicians, celebrities, athletes, and a loyal following. She staffed her restaurant with single mothers. For many years, she had the only upscale restaurant in New Orleans with an entirely female wait staff.

By the 1980s and 1990s, women were finding a path into business ownership. Whether it was Martha Stewart or Vera Bradley, the businesses they were opening and growing were providing new legitimacy for other women to start their own companies. The Women's Business Ownership Act was passed in 1988, ending discrimination for women in lending and eliminating laws that required married women to get their husband's signature on loans. And it gave women-owned businesses an opportunity to compete for government contracts.

By the 1990s, when Stephanie was looking at her career options, women were starting to establish themselves as success stories in the male-dominated world of entrepreneurship. Around that time, childcare was emerging as a growth industry. As Sandra L. Hofferth, a research scientist, writes, "Childcare was shifting from something only a few parents had to something that every parent needed." Driven by the number of women in the workforce, changes in marriages and divorce rates and family structures, and concerns among parents that their children have early childhood experiences, by the mid-1990s, 60 percent of children from birth through five years of age were with or in nonparental childcare or an early education program. That was over thirteen million children. It was becoming a new normal, and Stephanie decided to capitalize on it.

Meet Stephanie Breedlove

Stephanie Breedlove, founder of Breedlove & Associates and author of *All In: How Women Entrepreneurs Can Think Bigger, Build Sustainable Businesses, and Change the World*, found herself struggling with her career in a large corporate environment in the 1990s. She began her career when becoming a corporate player was just opening as a possibility for women.

Back then she wasn't even thinking about becoming an entrepreneur. Entrepreneurship was not a very acceptable option for women at the time. If you had children, you were supposed to stay at home and raise them. If you didn't like corporate life, you figured out how to endure it or maybe set up a small business. While entrepreneurship was emerging as a business opportunity for women, as were the laws to support women who wanted to open and run their new businesses, it was not considered a noble calling.

Stephanie's story is that of someone who saw her own life challenged and yet could also see solutions, problems to solve, and a way forward that might work for her, her family, and others around her. All along her journey, she was up-front and ready to take on the challenges. They didn't frighten her. Instead, they inspired her.

Stephanie grew up in Texas. Her father was the first in his family to attend college, and her mother was a traditional stay-at-home mom. As a child, Stephanie moved around a great deal as her dad pursued his corporate career. They settled down in Texas when her dad bought a hardware store in Bryan–College Station. Stephanie worked in the family store and graduated from high school in 1983 as one of seven valedictorians.

She went off to college at the University of Texas, getting a finance degree while reconnecting with Bill Breedlove, with whom she had been friends during her teen years. After graduation, they married and settled in Houston. Bill went to work for Tenneco, and Stephanie got her master's degree at the University of Houston.

When she completed her master's, she and Bill moved to Denver, where she landed a position at Accenture. Ironically, she was moving into business during a progressive time for women in corporate America. While men dominated the field, Stephanie thought the challenges facing her were part of a career pathway she was meant to travel. And she loved it. She thought a career at Accenture would take her the places she wanted to go—not as an entrepreneur but as a corporate success story.

At the time, she was part of that new breed of women going to college and entering the workforce not as executive secretaries, as teachers, as nurses, or even in staff roles but as career-driven professionals anxious to climb the corporate ladder to positions of importance and respect. Stephanie was on her way, as she thought she was supposed to be, with a significant place in a prestigious company. Smart, talented, and ambitious, she had crafted an excellent position at Accenture and seemed to be ready to move ahead on her journey.

When she discovered she was pregnant, she was able to negotiate with her boss a leave for five months, most of which was without pay. To her delight, she was granted this request and returned to Accenture to continue her work at the end of her leave. The only problem was that the new balancing act of wife, mother, and career professional was beginning to create more pain than pleasure for Stephanie, even with the generous salary and enriching job responsibilities.

Everything Stephanie was trying to accomplish was pushing the envelope on what society thought a woman should be doing. Stephanie soon realized that her job and the way the organization was structured were less fulfilling than she had imagined. She had that story in her head of everything working perfectly in tandem, but it just wasn't happening. While she had retained her position with the company, her curiosity and the ideas of her value had become boxed into her cubicle.

As she recalls, "I found myself wanting to participate more fully in solving business problems at work. Although I didn't yet have the title that would allow me to engage in solving problems comprehensively, I knew this was a skill and way of working that was important to me. Weighing in on only my small piece of the puzzle was frustrating. Being in a silo became a real negative of my corporate job."

Yet Stephanie knew that leaving her job and being focused solely at home wasn't an option she was willing to explore. Balancing the three roles led to changes, some of which were tolerable, and others were pushing the envelope. Stephanie and Bill realized their sons needed a great nanny who was a surrogate mother for them, offering additional support for Stephanie and Bill as they navigated the balancing act between family and careers. What they quickly realized was that having a nanny and paying her legally was more complicated than they initially realized. There were so many forms, procedures, deadlines, and legalities. And there did not seem to be a company they could turn to that could manage the paperwork, payroll, tax filing, and employment laws they needed. They knew they had a need to fulfill but did not know where to begin to solve it.

After much conversation and deliberation, they decided to see if others shared their frustrations and needs. That wanted to know if they were alone struggling with these problems or if this was something that needed a solution, perhaps one they could create. What Stephanie found, mainly talking to the agencies that placed the nannies, was that the mothers had no one to turn to for support. During her research, Stephanie went from "oh no" to "aha." I could almost feel the energy swish past me as she shared her story with me. That "aha" was an unanswered problem to solve: a curious perplexity, a simple question.

The questions Stephanie and her husband asked themselves were: What if more women returned to work long term and pursued careers? And what if we could start a service that helped these women with payroll, taxes, labor laws, contracts, and consultations?

The timing was rather fortuitous for Stephanie and Bill. They didn't sit around and dream of becoming successful entrepreneurs. Instead, they were struggling with a problem and realized that others like them were struggling too. So they decided to do something about it.

Stephanie did not take this grandiose leap as a given. She began slowly. As she shares, "It's usually a lot of pain and a slow process, and that's how it went for us. We built this little minimum viable product, and we delivered it on a very small scale in a couple of states as a test. We didn't quit our jobs. I was a career woman with young children, and now we had this little business on the side. We thought we were having fun, but then it began to grow legs. It started to have a little bit of traction, and we realized that a business on the side wasn't a recipe for success nor good for family life."

Stephanie recalls that she had reached that moment when she had to fish or cut bait. So she took the leap and left corporate America so she could take her start-up nanny-tax business idea national and to scale.

Breedlove & Associates launched in 1992 as a self-funded endeavor. Like so many women trying to start a new business venture, Stephanie did not have a network to tap into for angel investment or venture capital. And the banks were not ready to lend start-up funding. The idea that a woman was a reasonable business risk was counterculture at the time. Stephanie had a plan and the beginning of a business, with some revenue and no profits, so she went as fast as she could with limited resources. For entrepreneurs, this can be the most challenging part of growing a business. Or it can be precisely what it takes to launch and sustain the early-stage growth without having to accommodate other investors, family, or friends who are expecting a return on their angel funding or capital investments.

Stephanie jumped in with gusto and shouldered the new nanny-tax business for three years until her husband Bill decided to leave his corporate job and join her. When they sat down with her parents to tell them what Bill was doing, she got nothing but pushback. They had no models to refer to of other women who had succeeded in a start-up venture. Her parents could only see the doom and gloom that hard work and an early-stage company were going to offer them.

In spite of the pushback, they took the plunge and leaped forward. As with most businesses, they began to see a pattern emerge among the agencies with which they were collaborating. Clients came from those agencies that were placing the nannies. Together they were adding value for the parents and the nannies. Demand and revenue were growing.

At times, the hurdles seemed so high that it was difficult to see how they were going to overcome them, but Stephanie and her husband went from bootstrapping to turning around and building a business with enormous potential. From 1992 to 2012, Bill and Stephanie led Breedlove & Associates to serve tens of thousands of families in all fifty states. They helped these families process billions of dollars in household payroll and became the go-to experts in this highly specialized, exceedingly nuanced segment of tax and labor law. Hundreds of CPAs, financial managers, trust managers, and household staffing agencies began confidently referring clients to them for answers, advice, and service.

In 2012, Bill and Stephanie made another milestone decision to become part of Care.com, the world's largest online destination for finding and managing in-home care. It was a no-brainer for Care.com, as they saw millions of people across the country looking for care with no outlet for payroll, tax, or HR help once they had hired their staff. Breedlove had reached $9 million in annual sales and was growing. Care.com offered $39 million for Breedlove & Associates. After some careful thinking, Stephanie and Bill thought there was even more growth coming and turned down the offer. Marcelo then came back with a counteroffer, and they finally settled for $55 million, with half the purchase in cash and the remainder in Care.com stock—which goes to show what can happen when you offer a unique and in-demand service to an overlooked market. Stephanie is in good company with the other women in this book. As you read their stories, you will see how each of these women not only smashed the myths but also transcended them.

From the Observation Deck

As I shared Stephanie's story and that of her business, I was curious what lessons she had learned that would be relevant for others. As she looked back, she noted that some of the decisions worked well and others didn't. She had to build her staff, build a culture, and build processes. They were all anxiety-producing, yet she was able to turn the bootstrap company into a multimillion-dollar business.

And while it wasn't easy, Stephanie knew she had to change the way she was doing things to live the life she was meant to. So she defied the advice she received from her parents, because she knew that maintaining the status quo was not the life for her. I admire Stephanie's drive and determination. I have worked with people who knew they needed to change and yet were the same ones who most hated the idea, avoiding what they needed to do to move forward in their careers and their lives. In these instances, my counsel has typically been "If you want to change, have a crisis or create one." I say this because without the push to go beyond your habits and the story you carry in your mind about what is and what can be, you stay stalled, stuck in what is all too often a wrong place. In part, it is just your mind that fights these changes. And the antidote is the energy or catalyst that is needed to break past those habits and build new ones.

If you are going to build a business that is going to work, you are entering unknown territory with an idea in your head and a story to grow from it. The conversion of ideas to innovations, as Stephanie shares, "is some of the hardest work that you will ever do. It truly is, even if your calling is to be an entrepreneur, and it's absolutely the most fulfilling."

It takes courage to change and embark on a new journey. During our conversation, Stephanie said she and her husband focused on three strategies when growing their business, and we are sharing them with you here:

1. **They focused on the long-term strategies that built sustainable value.** They saw business building as a marathon and not a sprint.

2. **They embodied and embraced the philosophy that to have sustainable value, you have to build it right every time.** Because of this, they were committed to upholding high standards and consistent procedures and knew that training and skills development and systems and smart automation were pivotal. They also made good communication a priority so they could preserve the value of what they were creating.

3. **From the very beginning, they built their business with an intentional investment in the company culture as paramount to the strength and future of the company.** And everything flowed from there. As she says, "Culture first, and the rest will follow."

As a corporate anthropologist, I was fascinated by Stephanie's intentional focus on the culture of her organization. For Stephanie, her success came, in significant part, from a belief from the start that if you strive to bring out the best in people, then that brings out the best in your company.

As their company grew, Stephanie realized they had to hire people who would be enabled to grow out of their jobs. New employees had to have the self-starter skills and willingness to take some risks to build their capacity and add value to the organization. To enable them to sustain their development, Stephanie and Bill believed in training at every level, from new hires to those moving into new positions. Finally, they worked hard to set expectations and create accountability.

Often forgotten, Stephanie reminded me, is the importance of setting the bar and holding your people accountable to living according to those core principles. And it was this bar-setting and accountability that enabled Breedlove & Associates to grow from a struggling start-up to a multimillion-dollar company years after they took the entrepreneurial plunge.

Creating a successful business begins with a culture that can breed and nourish success. We tend to forget that what makes people "people" is their cultures and the stories they share while living their lives. If you don't create a culture in your company, people will make one up, and it will usually consist of a set of habits, beliefs, values, and behaviors that reflect what matters to them and not to you or your customers.

What was so exciting when I spoke with Stephanie was that she was sharing not only the great culture she created but also how to cultivate it. People embraced her culture and became part of it. They went all in and lived it. When a business does well, it is often because its culture has become their brand, and what you promise to your customers is also what you live every day and deliver at every touch point.

The philosophy of Breedlove & Associates was inclusive of its customers. Stephanie believes that you are only as valuable as the perception your clients have of your value. Their overarching company mission, which was at the backbone of their culture, was to be the undisputed experts in their space with a unique offering to maximize that value.

To achieve that goal, they had to have a culture of passionate people who believed and wanted to achieve the status of unparalleled expertise and service delivery. They also had to have a feedback loop from their clients to know that they were delivering on their promise and that their efforts were always improving, which makes a team proud and engaged. Stephanie wanted to have as comprehensive, efficient, and user-friendly a service as possible, which required engaging with and getting feedback from her clients.

Breedlove & Associates was a payroll and tax company. Yet it became an integral part of their clients' families by helping to guide a family through labor law and some of the sticky wickets. This level of service makes the difference in maintaining the employment relationship with someone who cares for your loved ones. As consultants,

Breedlove & Associates also wanted to be available for their clients, every step of the way. As Stephanie says, "Culture is something I believe is truly a secret to success." And I couldn't agree more. I hope you will draw inspiration from Stephanie's story to find a way to make your own unique culture the key to your success.

Women Are Not Good Leaders

"Leadership is hard to define, and good leadership
even harder. But if you can get people to follow you to
the ends of the earth, you are a great leader."

—*Indra Nooyi, CEO of PepsiCo*

There is a powerful myth out there that women do not make great leaders. It is a myth that has disturbed me my entire life. Girls learn early on who the guys are that others follow and what they need to do to get them to pay attention. Bold and decisive might be the rule for the men. Women, however, lead differently. They seek out team players and creative problem-solvers. Women mobilize their "followers" so organizations can move forward exponentially. They are visionaries and strive to empower others to facilitate and drive change. So if women can lead so successfully, why is this myth so widely protected? And why can't we see what is right before us: a great woman leader?

My husband, Andy (yes, we have the same name), and I have known Jamie Candee since 2014, the year she became president of Andy's company, Questar Assessment, a position she held until the company was sold in 2017. She did a remarkable job reigniting the growth of Questar and ultimately selling it to Educational Testing Services (ETS) with excellent returns to investors, and to my husband.

Back then Questar needed a new leader for a changing educational marketplace. Questar was growing rapidly as a company in the

K-12 summative assessment space. Andy knew that the then current president, Roy Lipner, had done some remarkable work building Questar, but it was time for a change in leadership. When they found Jamie Candee, Questar struck leadership gold.

Right away, Jamie accurately assessed what was working and what wasn't, and she instinctively knew how to move the company forward. As soon as she arrived, she rolled up her sleeves and got to work, pulling together a motivated team from current employees, hiring new talent with fresh skills, and building entirely new relationships with clients. Her strategy worked. Under Jamie's leadership, Questar grew by leaps and bounds, proving her leadership methods and business savvy were right on the money.

You're probably wondering how Jamie leads. Does she have an approach that combines an ability to engage with people, assess the gaps, and lead staff forward, both effectively and quickly? Or is she that creative leader who sees things with fresh eyes and can share her vision with others, mobilizing them to embrace the changes and her leadership? When you read her story, you'll learn that she's both.

The Myth

I always wanted to see a headline about Jamie Candee that read, "Creative Woman Makes a Great Leader." Throughout history we have witnessed the accomplishments of men as great leaders. Yet society has downplayed the leadership abilities of women. Men have been heralded as artistic geniuses, idea generators, visionaries, brilliant innovators, and builders of everything from tools to Sistine Chapels to major technological advances. However, when women tried to lead, they were seen as outliers who pushed the boundaries of where they belonged.

This downplay of women's successes reflects the societal norms and historical restrictions imposed upon women, not to mention the criticism (and ostracism) women have received if they veered too far from social conventions to become leaders. But from Victoria Woodhull—a leader of the women's suffrage movement and first woman to own a Wall Street brokerage firm and become a candidate for president of the United States—to Amelia Earhart, flying solo across the North Atlantic, there have always been women who have broken boundaries and demonstrated their innovative capabilities to lead others forward when the hurdles were high and the walls were set up to hold them back.

The reality, which research repeatedly shows us, is that women score as high if not higher than their male counterparts when leading or managing in a business. Jack Zenger and Joseph Folkman have conducted research on their database of 360 reviews to see how women rate when compared with men. In 2012, they discovered that "women in leadership positions were perceived as being every bit as effective as men. In fact, while the differences were not huge, women scored at a statistically significantly higher level than men on the vast majority of leadership competencies we measured."

In 2019 they found that "women are perceived by their managers—particularly their male managers—to be slightly more effective than men at every hierarchical level and in virtually every functional area of the organization. That includes the traditional male bastions of IT, operations, and legal."

While the research is based on managers' and staff's perceptions of men and women in leadership roles, the lingering biases are supporting stereotypes that don't match the realities of how women are leading and what they can do if given the chance. The problem, as described by Zenger and Folkman, is twofold: first, these women do not assume or assert they are that capable until they reach their forties, whereas the men are fast to present themselves as quite capable at an earlier stage in their careers. Second, the opportunities for women to progress into leadership roles is stymied by the management of companies, often men, who resist the idea that women can, in fact, be effective leaders—even if their employees rank them as every bit as strong as the men.

To further explain this dichotomy, Harvard Business School professor Amy Cuddy and her colleagues found that for women to succeed in business, they needed to combine "female" caring concern with "male" decisiveness in decision-making. They go further when they can build collaborative teams who trust their vision of the future and want to help them get there. Yes, female management styles *are* effective. They are often just quite different from how a man might lead.

Fortunately, the world appears to be catching up. Opportunities are expanding, albeit slowly, for women to take their energy and interests and turn them into successful business careers. And industry is beginning to capitalize on the creative energy, even genius, that women bring to their jobs, if allowed. Yet the number of women in senior leadership positions remains disturbingly low, relative to the talented women who are all around us.

Perhaps Jamie Candee's story can help bust this prevailing myth and inspire us to follow her lead. Her story shows us how we can shift our leadership style to different situations and have people follow us because they can see where they are going and how we are helping them get there. After all, isn't that what true leadership is all about?

Meet Jamie Candee

Jamie Candee is a perfect example of how women can lead successfully. Jamie has transformed every business she has led, as well as the way boards and others saw her as a CEO. Her skills grew over time and in different business situations where she developed her creative abilities. Over the course of her career, she has demonstrated how to take a start-up and help it grow, take a turnaround and make it soar, and take people and enable them to shine. Her style, skills, and successes offer a role model that others—male and female alike—should follow.

More importantly, Jamie forced people to challenge current definitions of creativity and innovation and how they come together in a woman leader, helping us see women succeeding in business through a new perspective. She truly understood when to be directing and when to be engaging and collaborative. She had a clear vision and built teams that eagerly followed her.

Jamie credits her success in great part to being a lifelong Curious George. She says she always wanted to know more about how and why something happened and would then use her findings to improve what she and others were doing. She has filled her life with bold ventures and effective business leadership, delivering the type of results often assumed to be the exclusive domain of men.

In Jamie's case, her story sheds light on what helped her achieve her style, confidence, and capabilities. While she says she was never sure exactly where she was going, she was always asking questions and searching for answers to satisfy her curiosity. There was no proverbial North Star toward which she was heading, but she was always on the move, forward.

And it all started when she was a young girl. Jamie was fortunate to have had supportive parents who taught her the importance of working hard and getting a good education. They had strong values but didn't push her into any particular career or job. They were hardworking people, raising a family while modeling how good people help their children and others.

Growing up in a small Minnesota suburb called Cottage Grove in the 1980s, Jamie was the first in her family to go to college. Her parents placed a great deal of value on education and worked hard to ensure she could get a college education, and she never forgot it. Not only did she work full time all the way through college, but the longest she took off from work in her entire life was when she had her first child, her son Milo.

For Jamie, her parents were the important role models that many successful women leaders need. Her dad worked all day, went to school at night, and helped care for two children under the age of eight. Her mom ran a hair salon twelve hours a day with ten employees. "I have always worked very, very hard, and I got that from my parents," Jamie says. "I think my parents were very successful, not from a monetary perspective, but from the values and the foundation they gave me to help me become who I am today."

In spite of the wonderful mentoring Jamie got from her parents, growing up was not easy. Struggling as a learner, she was placed in special education from kindergarten through the second grade, until she crossed paths with an exceptional teacher, Mrs. Rubright, who figured out how to teach her to read. Jamie's problem wasn't dyslexia but something else that kept her from identifying words and putting them together. With Mrs. Rubright's help, Jamie went from barely reading at the second-grade level to reading at an advanced level only one year later.

Jamie credits Mrs. Rubright with not only teaching her to read but igniting in her a love for creatively solving problems that seem unsolvable, along with an appreciation of the power of teachers and learning.

As Jamie grew up, she mimicked her mother and began to try out entrepreneurial ideas. One summer, she decided she was going to open a restaurant. She took her parents' groceries, which they had worked so hard to buy, and opened a "restaurant," selling sandwiches to everyone in the neighborhood. Her free spirit got her into trouble as she was growing up, but the bold, risk-taking, creative entrepreneur was emerging.

Jamie's first "real" job was detasseling corn. Imagine what you learn working in ninety-degree heat, pulling tassels off corn with bugs swarming all around you. Even as a kid, Jamie knew the value of hard work, tackling every task with grit, determination, and persistence— lessons that have stayed with her. Each job was a training ground, expanding her personal skills, her belief in herself, and her vision of what she could become. Starting with her neighborhood restaurant, she was always ready to push the envelope and was never too concerned about what might happen if she did.

Although Jamie had an opportunity to attend the University of Wisconsin–Madison, she went to the smaller University of Wisconsin–River Falls instead, the education-focused campus of the UW system. With the goal of becoming a teacher, she made it through her undergraduate program and into student teaching when she realized she loved children and might even love teaching, but she couldn't imagine herself in a classroom. The classroom experience taught Jamie that she was more curious about the effects of education policy on classroom instruction.

What did she do? She pivoted. She changed her major to political science, thinking she would go to law school instead. She was admitted to law school but ran out of money while she was finishing up her undergraduate degree, as she was paying for her own education. Undeterred, she found an internship at a bank that paid well enough for her to start thinking about law school again while she continued with her undergraduate studies.

After her banking internship, Jamie worked as a teller, then moved into business banking. When she graduated from college, she accepted an offer to join an apprenticeship program to become a commercial lender with a regional bank trying to expand its Small Business Association (SBA) program.

Jamie recalls, "This was a great experience. It was my first opportunity to really understand how few women and minorities at that time were running companies and how this bank could be a catalyst for funding so these folks could get their businesses up and running."

And then the unexpected happened, something that would change the trajectory of Jamie's career path. While doing commercial lending for an entrepreneur client who had launched a new financial services business, the client asked Jamie to help him develop his start-up. She was twenty-one. She took the job, which became a training platform that enabled her to learn more than she ever imagined about running a business.

During her four years at the start-up, Jamie learned about business in all its different dimensions, from mergers and acquisitions to human resources to how to build an organization from scratch to how to drive a sales organization. She also learned what it was like to be accountable for operations. The experience couldn't have been better. Not everyone can dive into a new entrepreneurial company and build it while they're running it, but Jamie did.

Some people might stay in a company like this and grow with it, but Jamie got burned out. She examined what she really loved and what she had done to get the job completed. She kept returning to her interest in leadership, leadership development, talent recruitment, and human resource management. After some careful consideration, she decided it was a good time to leave the young company and thanked it for allowing her to learn what was to become the foundation of her approach to building businesses.

Her interests took her to the human resources division of a staffing company, Pro Staff. She became an employee relations and leadership development consultant, both of which touched upon her deeper interest in how a company's culture and its people interact to create an organization that can grow.

Being a creative entrepreneur, Jamie realized that the company was handling all the recruiting for large international companies with foreign corporate headquarters. They were performing the function of an HR department but were not being paid as such. After noticing this gap, she went to work fixing the business model, turning the company into an outsourced HR service and embedding its HR team into other companies.

Before long, Jamie had an "aha" moment. As she tells it, "I realized, you know what? I want to run companies. I want to lead people. I'm really interested in getting back to being a lifelong learner."

She discovered that when she hired the right people and developed them properly, they became engaged and motivated. Those engaged employees were the people who built her businesses. She just had to harness that energy with a laser focus and spread it throughout an entire company. She learned that she could lead only if others would follow. And this would not happen through autocratic, decisive directing. She had to make others *want* to follow her, rather than force them.

As well as focusing on bringing along the right people, Jamie began to appreciate the importance of an organization's culture and creating the right leadership to match the culture. She learned that her leadership styles could shift as her roles changed in different organizations, which led to an unusual opportunity that would synthesize all the things she had been learning and building up to.

In the early 2000s, technology was beginning to move into education, which piqued Jamie's curiosity. She became interested in how technology and the digital world were engaging with kids and teachers. At the time, PLATO Learning, Inc. (now called Edmentum after rebranding in 2012) was entering this education space. When Jamie had the opportunity to join the organization as their human resources manager, she jumped at it. And she came full circle, returning to her early and enduring interest in kids, teachers, and talent development. Over the course of almost nine years, she ran every part of the organization, eventually rising to the position of chief revenue officer.

In 2014, Jamie wasn't ready to leave Edmentum, but she was ready to become a CEO. Her daughter was three months old when Jamie got a call from Questar Assessment, my husband's company.

Questar was looking for a new CEO, since my husband, who had founded and grown the company, was ready to move into the chairman's role and find new leadership to take the company to the next stage in its growth.

Questar was a wonderful company, small at the time, with great people, a forward-looking mission, and a positive culture, but it needed to focus on growth. Jamie decided to take Questar up on their offer and join them as their new CEO. Yes, it was hard in the beginning, and yes, she had a lot of work to do to get the company on a growth track, mainly because the industry was changing so dramatically. But she did it.

To stay relevant, the company needed to make investments in assets, products, services, and, most of all, people. Over the next three years, Jamie hired new talent and built a highly engaged team that wanted to do great things for education and help grow a business. And it worked. Questar grew and grew and was sold to ETS in March of 2017.

After that, Edmentum called her—the board wanted her to return as their CEO! The timing was perfect, and she is now back at Edmentum and absolutely thrilled to be there.

As of 2019, Jamie is two years into her role as president and CEO of Edmentum, a leading provider of online learning programs to improve student achievement. Under her watch, she and her team (and she always refers to the team) have had remarkable successes, even after the company's three years of flat performance before she rejoined it and helped it grow.

You may be wondering: What's the secret to her leadership success? Jamie would say it's simple: take the complex and tell it in a simple story so people see it, understand it, and know where they are going. Then they buy it and follow you.

As Jamie told me during our conversations, one of the principles she learned early on from her mentors is that even if you're running only one small part of the business, you should do everything you can to learn all aspects of the company. This is how you get the whole picture and can, in turn, distill it into a relatable message for each team in your company. She recalls early on how she would ask each department if she could shadow them to learn what they did, whether it was sitting in on marketing meetings, going out on sales calls, or sitting in the call center, listening to customer calls. This curiosity and desire to learn as much as she could about every part of the whole enabled her to see the greater picture while also honing in on the smaller details. By learning how all the interconnected pieces of the companies worked and fit together, she could then use this knowledge to motivate and inspire her employees in each of the businesses she led.

From the Observation Deck

Jamie, along with many of the successful women whose stories I am sharing in this book, is not only curious but also observant. She watches what people do, how they converse with each other, how they solve problems or don't, and how they build cultures that support the growth of the organization, not just the individual.

Part of the reason Jamie has been successful is because she always looks at the business from the outside in. She wonders what her clients are thinking and doing and what she and her staff can do to help them. She firmly believes "if you bring together culture and customer, you can get a very good perspective on the entirety of the business. Then watch your employees work. Just sit with them and watch the way they communicate and how they collaborate. That can give you a very good sense of the entire organization."

Another key to her success comes from viewing the business as one ecosystem. Her clients were inseparable from what the company was doing, and you cannot ask your clients to change to better align with your company. You have to change the organization serving those clients. And you must see both sides as one. Your company becomes part of the daily life of your clients. Then you can lead them both forward.

I have always preached to clients that strategy is a simple story that helps people understand where you are going and how you are going to get there. Jamie understood that and realized this was her role. She has always been able to see the forest for the trees. She seems to always know where to take an organization for the next three to five years, then how to break down that larger objective into two or three goals that need to be done each year to achieve the longer-term plan. And regardless of which company she has worked with, she has managed to find colleagues to work with her who are smart and capable and complement her skills. Finally, she overdetermines success by constantly discussing with employees why they are doing what they are doing and how it is going to get them where they need to go.

In Jamie's case, at each stop along the way she saw an opportunity, as much to learn as to do, and took it. Some worked out better than others, but at each stop the organizations had major challenges to solve and needed a leader who was not afraid of crafting a new way of solving problems to move forward.

You might wonder, where does it start? Do successful women become effective, creative leaders all at once, or is this something that starts early on in their lives? Wanting to better understand how women find their way into leadership roles, the professional services firm KPMG surveyed 3,014 US women (2,410 professional working women and 604 college women) between the ages of eighteen and sixty-four. KPMG found that, like Jamie, the women in the survey learned how to take charge and own their success during childhood. This was when those values were being taught. They were exposed to people who demonstrated effective leadership styles, and they were inspired to take on leadership roles even when young.

Second, being around strong professionals who encouraged them to take risks and to rise above the ordinary helped shape their view of how to lead in a workplace setting. They all had mentors who let them try things, as well as experiences that built their confidence.

What also became apparent in the KPMG study was that women needed other women if they were to grow their self-confidence and find the right leadership styles to use in different situations. Women fear the isolation that comes with leadership positions if there is no network of peers who can become their community, their shared culture, and their support team.

Whether it was working in her mother's salon, detasseling corn, starting a restaurant, or driving friends around town for a fee, Jamie knew what she wanted and what she had to do to get it. She even overcame her learning limitations (with Mrs. Rubright's help). Now Jamie is helping other women find their own paths. She urges them to take some risks and, most importantly, to learn from their mistakes. While often scary, she says these risks help you discover your strengths. And then hopefully, a great opportunity will come your way and you'll seize it. And take off running.

Women Cannot
Run a Fashion Business

"I don't like to talk about my dreams.
I like to make them happen."

—*Diane von Fürstenberg*

Babette Ballinger's story is that of a woman who grew into a successful clothes designer, manufacturer, and marketer of apparel—first in childrenswear, then in womenswear, and eventually establishing her own brand of Babette Ballinger knitwear. As she told me her story, her life was a reflection of the significant transformation in the US garment industry from the late 1960s into the early part of the twenty-first century, and the challenges faced by a woman trying to build a career in an industry run by men. Like Diane von Fürstenberg, Babette had dreams and made them happen, albeit not in a straight line from start to finish.

Her story begins in the early 1960s. Women were still minorities in the garment industry and only beginning to work in design positions. Few women were retail buyers. The only jobs available were as the assistant to the assistant. As the 1970s approached, women started to feel freer. There was some choice in jobs, and this translated to choice in how you dressed and then the explosion of the junior youth market of the 1970s.

From then on, everything seemed to be changing in the garment industry: retailing, consumers, garments, design, and technology. The men didn't understand this freedom expressed by young women, and the junior designers were young girls. Manufacturing began to migrate overseas to lower-cost producers, mostly in the Far East, as American manufacturers struggled to hold on to their businesses back home. Fabrics were changing as synthetics entered the market. Retailing was facing new competitors as catalogs challenged stores, and department stores challenged each other. Those women consumers were entering the workforce and changing their clothes every day, and they wanted those clothes to be affordable and stylish. They were less concerned with their durability than their low cost and high-quality stylishness. Even kids' clothes were changing as little girls discarded their pretty little dresses for sportswear they could play in.

I've known Babette for a long time. She and my husband went to Washington University in St. Louis in the early 1960s. Babette was in the design school, and Andy played football. They met in the cafeteria at odd hours, because she would be cutting and sewing garments long into the night while he was getting free meals in the cafeteria after football practice. Then, by chance, she bought a home close to ours, and we became longtime friends. It was such a pleasure to listen to her tell me her story and to better understand how a woman could overcome the hurdles and smash through the challenges before her in the garment industry that was less than welcoming to "smart" women. She had a challenging career. Her journey is one that will inspire those young women coming out of fashion schools today and give them hope that they, too, can smash that Glass Runway and build the types of personal and professional careers they aspire to achieve.

The Myth

In the latter half of the 1960s, when Babette was entering the garment industry, a severe disruption was underway in the US. Everything seemed to be changing. Before the Second World War, the US had global dominance in garment manufacturing with over two million jobs. After the war, accelerating in the 1970s, changes were coming both to where garments were manufactured and in the design of those garments.

In 1960, an average American household spent over 10 percent of its income on clothing and shoes. The average person bought fewer than twenty-five garments each year. About 95 percent of those clothes were US made. By 2000, the average American household spent less than 3.5 percent of its budget on clothing and shoes. Yet they bought more clothing than ever before, with nearly 20 billion garments a year, close to seventy pieces of clothing per person, or more than one clothing purchase per week. Of that, only about 2 percent was made in the US.

As a result, the entire garment industry and particularly the marketing associated with it were changing. The ease with which people could buy mass-produced garments and the speed with which they could change their wardrobes demanded faster production and less expensive clothes. Dramatic innovations were shifting the supply chain, challenging the structure, scope, and scale of garment manufacturers. Synthetic fibers were replacing natural cotton, silk, and wool. Many hoped that new technologies would be panaceas for the industry to help modernize production and reduce the cost of goods. Productivity in the apparel assembly line was advancing, as computers could assist in labor-intensive material management, and robotic sewing could hopefully bring new ways to assemble garments that would reduce the need for labor. Union labor had raised the cost of production in ways that challenged the sustainability of the manufacturing sector in the US.

The relatively low cost of imported products created severe stress for the garment industry. By 1985, when measured in square yards, 33 percent of the US textile market and 48 percent of the US apparel market was imported, more than doubling since 1975. The projection at that time was that by 2000, no apparel would be manufactured in the US, and they were almost correct.

In the mid-1970s throughout Asia, emerging markets were building large textile mills and factories. These operations offered incredibly cheap labor and raw materials. They could also quickly manufacture large orders.

To be competitive, manufacturers became importers but still controlled the design process. As retail operations consolidated and then became public entities, they needed to do away with the manufacturers as middlemen and start doing the bulk of importing and design themselves.

A growing number of big retail chains like Gap Inc. and J. C. Penney began transitioning away from domestic importers and instead hired their own designers and established their own importing departments. They outsourced production to factories overseas where the cost of goods was a fraction of what it was in the US.

Meanwhile, those same companies developed vast global supply chains that allowed them to divide up each step of the production process, sending the work to whichever location offered the cheapest, most efficient services. By 2003, "Gap was ordering its clothes from more than 1,200 different factories in 42 countries," according to Elizabeth Cline, author of *Overdressed: The Shockingly High Cost of Cheap Fashion.*

Today, more and more women are running significant companies in the fashion industry. In fact, women are now leading almost 40 percent of the major fashion houses in the C-suite. In smaller companies, women are quickly pushing forward. And the internet has enabled many women to open their brands, manage manufacturing in the Far East, and build marketing and sales solutions that leverage e-commerce and social media. We can look to Diane von Fürstenberg and Donna Karan, Ellen Tracy and Liz Claiborne, Anne Klein, Tory Burch, and Maureen Chiquet. And their numbers are growing. Despite these women's influence, this is still an industry run by men.

Women have been able to progress up to middle management in the fashion industry. However, the gender inequality at the C-suite is profound. About 85 percent of the graduating class of fashion majors is women, whether from Parsons, Fashion Institute of Technology, or Pratt. At Pratt, fifty-four of the fifty-eight graduating fashion majors in 2018 were women. While they, like Babette, all knew they were going to have to start their careers with entry-level positions, they still had high aspirations to become "stars" in this industry.

The Glass Runway study conducted by and released in 2019 by the CDFA, Glamour, and McKinsey found that 100 percent of the women interviewed said there was gender discrimination and inequality in fashion, while less than 50 percent of men thought there was a problem. Thirty-seven percent of the men thought their company was addressing the gender-biased language, while only 17 percent of the women believed their company was doing anything about it.

Another force was also at work influencing how women were engaged in this industry. We must remember that even today, gender can negatively affect what we think about the quality of products designed and built by women. The recurring myth is that women are not as creative as men and that they certainly cannot run a business. Unfortunately, that perspective has not changed dramatically. As Stanford researchers Sarah Soule, Elise Tak, and Shelley Correll found in their study of goods made by women, regardless of the type of product, if people think a woman made it, they believe it is not as good as if a man made it. When consumers believed a woman produced a product, they claimed they would pay less for it, and they had lower expectations for its tastes or its functionality or value.

This gender bias easily extended to all types of endeavors. What's worse is that research suggests that even women think men are more creative, and they associate creativity with more masculine traits such as risk-taking, independence, and daring. Women and tasks done by women reflect their more sensitive and caring nature. Research on house designs, for example, found that women and men rated creativity higher when told that a man did the design.

Further, the language we use biases us toward how we "feel" about the work of men and women. In 2015, Allyson Stokes, a sociologist at the University of Waterloo, did in-depth research about how men and women are recognized by their fashion industry, the Council of Fashion Designers of America (CFDA). Her research highlighted the problem with fashion—as well as with art, film, and music—in that people don't know how to judge something when there are no standards or objective guidelines to use. Without that standard, there is no set of rules to capture the quality of a design. Most perceptions and judgments are then based on their brain's own confirmation biases.

Research in psychology, sociology, and other social sciences says when people make decisions when they are uncertain or ambiguous, they end up falling back on their biases, stereotypes, and traditional ideas. The words we choose and the perceptual maps in our brains take over. Language is particularly relevant here. When Stokes analyzed her data, she found the language used to describe a fashion designer as "great" relied on gendered stereotypes. Men and the product of their work is viewed as autonomous, rational, independent, creative—whereas women are seen in our brain's stories as quiet, tiny, calm, or unable to commit fully to their craft. As Stokes adds, "When we use those kinds of terms without recognizing the gender assumptions behind them, we end up (even if we're not trying to) creating an image of what it means to be a great designer that is subtly, implicitly, but definitely gendered."

These were the challenges that faced Babette in the 1960s. In her story, you will learn how she found success in an industry run by men. As we spoke, she reminded me of what we would like to tell all of those recent graduates with design degrees hoping to achieve fame and fortune. Babette doesn't think about the hurdles she had to climb or the obstacles she had to overcome. Instead, she tells a story about how you can succeed even in an industry dominated by men, where you can still be a woman, have a family, and find success.

Meet Babette Ballinger

In some ways, Babette's journey followed the path of her grandmother, whom Babette never knew. Babette found out much later that her grandmother had been a dressmaker and designer in Germany, with forty women working for her, serving the very best customers. When she immigrated to New York in the early 1900s, Babette's grandmother opened her own couture dress business in her home. Before the ready-to-wear clothing that is mass-produced today, you either bought the fabric and made your dress at home on your Singer sewing machine, or you had a dressmaker make the pieces for you.

Babette's parents were not in the fashion business, and Babette could not turn to anyone as a role model or a mentor. Babette's parents lived in New York. Her mother was getting her doctoral degree in microbiology at Hunter College. Her father played professional baseball for the New York Giants' farm team and then professionally for a short season around 1944–1945, when the great players were at war and the lesser players were promoted to keep the sport going. It was a time when you could make the team and play your heart out but not make a lot of money. Following his baseball stint, Babette's dad had neither a job nor any schooling, so he decided to become a legal secretary, recording the proceedings of legal meetings. When he finished his training, first in his class, he discovered that in New York, he would have to work for the court system. But in Tennessee, he could open his own business. So when Babette was three years old, her family moved to Memphis.

What they learned rather quickly was that women did not work in Tennessee. And if they did, it was as a nurse, a teacher, or a secretary. Her mother had a degree and was studying for her doctorate. Rather than fuss over the inequities, she became a volunteer supporting the Jewish school, the PTA, and other organizations that were important for their community and for her own sanity. Her father became a successful court recorder, and together they raised their two daughters.

When it came time for Babette to head to college, she had to find a place with a program she would like. She knew she was a good artist, and fashion illustration was something she was interested in pursuing. She knew she didn't want to teach or become a nurse. This was the 1960s; women did not have a lot of options. A teacher suggested she apply to Washington University in St. Louis, which had a commercial art, education, and fashion design program. She checked off fashion design, not really knowing what it offered. Somehow, she ended up spending four years at college sewing. Babette was miserable, but she couldn't transfer, so she stuck it out. They didn't even let her take a year of art, business, or the humanities. She just sewed her way through college. Ironically, she was in great demand. Every time dresses or costumes were needed for a Bearskins Folly or other event, the dress designers were the go-to solution, and all night long, she sewed. So she made the most of it.

After she graduated, Babette returned to New York. She was all set for her first adventure in the city, 1960s Jackie Kennedy–style, with her dress, hat, and gloves, and she happily walked down the streets as the guys would hoot at her. Her first job lasted a week. The second one lasted two weeks. At the next one, the guy had fired his designer and promoted the next person in line. Babette came in and became the second-string designer. Within no time, the head designer who had been fired called her up and asked her to join her start-up business.

Babette went to work in this kidswear start-up. It was a good fit for her, since she always wanted to be in the childrenswear industry. During this time, mothers still dressed up their children, and girls wore beautiful dresses. Some companies had great designers for children's clothes, many of whom were women. Babette saw them as stars. This success was what Babette wanted to achieve. She started working with Kate Greenway, the children's dress manufacturer, as the dress designer for the 7 to 14 sizes. These were the days of knit dresses, and here she was in her early twenties, on her way.

Then her mother died in a freak car accident. Babette was devastated but knew she had to move on. She went to another company, where the owner screamed all the time and treated everyone terribly. After a few months, Babette couldn't take it. She went to work for another company, Richling, Ades & Richling (RAR), and the label she did was called Moppets. RAR was a well-run company with a vast 7 to 14 business, and Babette learned a lot. She was growing into a successful designer in the kidswear industry. More importantly, she was learning how to run a business.

As she reflected on her time there, "I had worked for all the best childrenswear companies, but the writing was on the wall to me that kids aren't wearing pretty little dresses anymore, and everything else was changing. I mean, we worked on children's clothes with the Sesame Street license. I did little purses with all the little animals. It was really creative. I had two women, one who sewed and one who embroidered, working for me. I didn't have to touch a sewing machine, which was perfect. And I was earning fairly good money at the time. I went from $60 a week to $150 a week. It was a lot of money then."

All the moving around was part of the culture. As Babette changed companies, she kept building her skills, her reputation, and her vision for what she was going to do in this industry. But she was ready for some time off to rethink who she was and what mattered to her.

Around this time Babette decided to travel to Europe and Israel. Wanderlust had set in. She was twenty-four, her sister had married, her mother had died, and she loved designing for the best kidswear companies. She had worked on great licenses like Sesame Street, and she was making good money. But she had to wonder, was that all there was? She didn't know what was to come next. She just knew she had to get out of New York.

So off she went with her copy of *Europe on $5 a Day*, traveling all across Europe and Israel, living frugally, staying at people's homes and with others she met as she traveled. To her amazement, she loved to talk to people and found it easy to meet them. They each seemed to teach her something about life and herself, like a mirror that allowed her to see inside herself while opening the door to the outside. Her experience and her career had been a straight line until then, with little direction and a great deal of change. She knew she needed goals. Her designer approach was always to see what the end product—the goal—was and then design it to achieve that objective. Babette had to do the same for herself.

When she returned to the US, it had become a different country. Vietnam was escalating. The Kennedy brothers and Martin Luther King had been assassinated. Babette was unsure of what was next but realized that it didn't matter. She was designing her own life, not simply the clothes for kids to wear.

Soon after, Babette went to work with guys she had known who were starting a T-shirt dress company in Long Island City. But the area was unsafe, so, at the urging of a friend, she decided to move to California. Babette got offered a job at a sweater company, Organically Grown, and even though she had never made a sweater before, the company paid for her moving expenses. They found her a house, met her at the airport, and before she knew it, she was on her way to a profitable and fun venture.

Through her astute lens, Babette was figuring out what was going on in every part of the business and where they were making their goods. From the perspective of the guys she was working with, she was becoming too smart. The owners thought Babette was asking too many questions, and they didn't appreciate being questioned. Babette had become a great sweater designer, but they wanted this too-smart lady out. She turned around one day to find her car and perks gone, and she was left wondering what to do.

Babette shopped around and kept hearing that the place to work was Bronson of California. Bob and Lee Bronson had a developing business and were thinking about manufacturing abroad. Babette went to talk to one of the brothers, Lee Bronson, and during their chat he said, "I am hiring you." When he asked her what salary she required, she made up a number that seemed to make sense and started work the next day.

The head designer at Bronson of California was a young black woman, Patty Davis Evans, who asked Babette to do the soft garments. Bob Bronson, the other brother, said they "were grossing $7 million and wanted to get to $100 million. I think we have to go overseas. We will figure this out. I want you, because you are smart." It was, as she recalls, the first time anyone hired her because of her smarts, and it mattered. Babette was now more than a gal who could design something. She knew the business and could help the Bronsons grow theirs.

Between them, they built Bronson of California from $7 million to $100 million in gross revenues. Those were the early days of polyester suits. Babette's vision was to create a category where all the pieces could work together. She put everything you could into the creation of shirts and suits, with color-related separates that could mix and match. Her vision was to have "black, navy, and brown basics and then the polyester suits in fashion colors of rust, teal, and burgundy, with tops that were tone-on-tone, mixed with the basic colors."

She recalled fondly, "With the prints, we would mix them up, and you could get a reasonable number of units that would all go together. We could use the same fabrics, and things wouldn't get dated. It was a very revolutionary approach with color-related separates. This was also in the heyday of nylon-printed shirts. Every friend I had was doing the print designs with me, and we were putting all kinds of motifs on them from art deco toilets to matchbook covers and Mucha prints."

The Bronson strategy was smart. They would have one salesman rent rooms at the Hotel Pierre. Female models would walk around with the suits on as if it were a couture brand. Bronson would get the stores to commit to the A, B, or C packages, which was easier for business building. These polyester suits were a hit, a tool that spurred creative ideas to grow the company.

Babette was with Bronson for five years as the merchandiser for the brand. She did the concepts and general designs for the sweaters, the argyles, and the stripes, and had people working for her. Her job was like running an art studio, so amazingly creative. Babette didn't think about the money she was making. The Bronsons treated her like family. Then the times started to change. Bob decided that his pretty young girlfriend was a better designer than Babette. When the girlfriend vied for her job, Babette began to think about the next phase in her journey.

Always open to possibilities, Babette went to India with another company to see what they could do to develop a business. To avoid difficulties with tariffs, they were shipping to Bangladesh. While she enjoyed the journey, Babette felt unfulfilled in her career. She eventually moved back to California to work for another company, Montage and Collage. Soon after that, she got a call from a head-hunter to see if she wanted to go to New York to start a division for Bobbie Brooks.

Babette jumped at the opportunity. While in New York look-ing for a place to live, she met Raymond Ballinger, her husband to be. They met in 1980 and married two years later. Raymond was an actor working on daytime soaps, commercials, and parts in films. He noticed Babette's travels were wearing her down. After a miscarriage, they decided it was time for her to start her own company and stay closer to home, which was particularly crucial after their daughter, Rebecca, was born in 1987.

For Babette, the timing was perfect. In 1984 she launched Babette and Partners, a domestic knitwear company that flourished until 1989. She loved the autonomy. Her future was now in her own hands. She could be as successful as her talents allowed her to be. Babette and Partners continued to grow, but she began to realize she didn't want partners. So in 1992, she started American Knitworks to build a more mass-market sweater line and the more high-end Babette Ballinger knitwear label.

A friend of a friend came to her and said they had a domestic mill that wasn't doing well, reflecting the fast-melting tip of the iceberg for domestic manufacturing that was rapidly moving overseas. The guy said, "Look, if you use it and make the factory work, terrific, and if you can't, we're going to close it down. It's not been doing well for a long time. Do what you can." The other factories they owned were in North Carolina and Pennsylvania. They had many dye plants and specialized in dying, tie-dying, and embroidery. They also did private label work for Victoria's Secret and Guess.

Babette took him up on the offer and also continued to grow her own business. Her experience had taught her a great deal. She knew she had to come up with a unique product, since the stores couldn't do that for themselves and relied on their buyers. Babette reached out to stores' buying offices. While she had not done much in sales, she knew the other buyers were also young women.

Around 1996, Babette realized it was time to go back to being her own boss without partners. She had a company with $6 to $8 million in business and three factories that had goods in progress. Of course, she didn't have much capital to invest. So she went to CIT and Rosenthal & Rosenthal—two well-known factors lending garment manufacturers against their unpaid invoices—to get funding. With her clean balance sheet and her smarts, they gave her significant financing proposals. With CIT as her factor, she was back in her own business.

Babette was now developing her line of sweaters. American Knitworks and the Babette Ballinger's sweater line were in business from 1992 to 2008, with revenues exceeding $20 million. Her designs were featured in specialty stores and department stores, including Stern's, Bamberger's, Macy's, Bonwit Teller, Saks Fifth Avenue, Marshall Fields, and others. She also had her catalog business with J.Jill, Coldwater Creek, Appleseeds, TravelSmith, and Victoria's Secret and shipped under their label or private labels for these catalogs. Babette Ballinger was the better-priced, more sophisticated line, while American Knitworks was more volume oriented—terrific quality with excellent design and fit at a great price.

Throughout her journey, Babette repeatedly reinvented herself. Toward the end, she decided she didn't want to carry inventory. So she gave up the specialty stores and stuck with the catalogs, which she enjoyed the most. As the catalog business began to change, she kept winding down her own business. People didn't want to buy her business. They still just wanted to buy Babette. But it was time to execute her exit strategy, and she never looked back.

From the Observation Deck

In so many ways, Babette's journey was that of the garment industry in the postwar period from the 1960s into the early twenty-first century. Hers was the life of the smaller businesses, family firms, and start-ups, each trying to compete as the department stores rolled up, catalogs expanded, and manufacturing went to lower-cost global centers. She saw the changes coming and was able to leverage her skills and smarts to capitalize on them.

Part of Babette's success can be attributed to her ability to reinvent herself over and over again. She was always a gifted, talented designer. And then she became an equally skilled businesswoman who took over fashion businesses that men were unable to run profitably. Her journey raised many of the central questions we have today about how a woman can thrive in an industry that is controlled by men. It isn't that different now for all those talented women coming out into the fashion industry who are looking for more than just a job. Like Babette, they want a career and control.

Unfortunately, women's relationship with men in the fashion industry then and even today has women doing the work, creating the designs, sewing the garments, and only reluctantly being allowed to run the business. Only the guys, they say, know how to run the business. Funny how the owners of those failing factories offered them to Babette when they were at a loss to how to run them profitably. She was their last chance, and then they all walked away from a remnant of the past when America had productive manufacturing here.

Several important themes emerge from Babette's life story:

1. **The language we use and the stories we tell must change.**
   The first is the way we think about men and women and their creativity. Language is not incidental to the problem. In some ways, the way we think about the design and capabilities of men

and women leads us to the myths we use. We like to put them in each of their boxes: men and their creative designs are seen as strong, decisive, and positive, whereas women's designs are viewed as more subdued, subtle, and caring. The research is disturbing, because it is as relevant today as it was a hundred years ago. The stories have to change, and the women who are leading the way are helping to improve it. But the men who control the media must also change their perception of women and of men to craft a more balanced mythology.

This great transformation and equalization are complicated. In 2017, at the annual CFDA awards, men were nominated for both top menswear and womenswear awards. While the industry is still called a feminized occupation, the men still cannot embrace the achievements of these accomplished women.

And at the 2019 Advertising Week events, with an overall theme about the empowerment of women, the closing night entertainment blew it all apart. While there may have been panel discussions all week long about "Mom Bosses" and "#Rewrite-HerStory," the rapper Pitbull ended the week with the hit "I Like It" with female dancers in bodysuits surrounding him as he sang about wanting to "play" with women.

These industries seem glued to their sexist pasts and are reluctantly offering no better than lip service to women to smooth their ruffled feathers and create the illusion that the mythology and the reality are changing.

2. **Women need women to help them build their businesses. And part of that starts with helping young girls believe in themselves.** Babette was in a highly competitive environment with few mentors to help her along her way. Women need their role models and teammates. They also need to believe that each woman can achieve her aspirations even if dreams don't always come true.

Of equal importance, women need to learn about how to run a business from women running those businesses. A certain vocabulary and style is necessary, and it is not the same as a man's. But it works, albeit differently. And it is OK to be different.

I love the programs devoted to teaching young women and girls all about entrepreneurship. Most importantly, the research is showing us that women kick butt when they run a business. Some organizations are encouraging women to mentor other women about business and about themselves. And there is no shortage of online support for women with ideas to turn into successful business innovations.

In many ways, the world that Babette knew has exploded, offering women today a much bigger space in which to find others like themselves and the support network to help them thrive. But you don't want to do it all alone. Women need others and a community to support them.

3. **Men can be great teammates, mentors, and partners.** Babette teamed up with Bob Bronson to help him grow his business. She had some great men as mentors, such as at RAR, to teach her all about business. And she had those who saw her as a smart woman and then helped her grow. As much as mentoring has become an essential part of becoming a successful woman in businesses, finding the right mentor or being one is not as easy as you might imagine.

What research is discovering is that many women don't ask for mentoring and are not sure how to be mentored. And even those who want to become mentors are awkward at delivering support for others. That is a problem as much for men as mentors as it is for women mentoring other women. Part of our transformation is in becoming skilled and comfortable at helping each other. Women must stop feeding the backbiting assumed to characterize female relationships.

Regardless of where you are in your own journey, remember that you must see the future to achieve it. If you can see it, you can get there. As Babette says, "Believe in yourself and never let go of the end goal. Be agile and willing to reinvent yourself and your product, always changing with the times." Your goal should be less a destination than a great journey with twists and turns moving you closer, with each step, to the life you were meant to live.

Women Shouldn't Be Lawyers

"Whenever you see a successful woman, look out for three
men who are going out of their way to block her."

—*Yulia Tymoshenko, leader of the
All-Ukrainian Union "Fatherland" political party*

When I was nineteen and met my husband on Schroon Lake in the
Adirondacks, he asked me what I wanted to be. I told him that I was
either going to be an anthropologist or an attorney. He quickly said,
"Oh, be an anthropologist, and I will be here for you."

Well, I am an anthropologist and not at all sorry I did not go
into law. But women don't have an easy time in either profession. I
would have needed my husband with me one way or the other. So
did Andrea (Andie) Kramer, who needed her husband, Al Harris.
Without his support, she would never have been able to become a
successful lawyer, parent, and member of the communities that she
is so involved with today. Yet Andie didn't need just a husband to
take care of her. She needed a partner to share her journey, celebrate
her accomplishments, and join together to help other women achieve
similar success.

In 2020, there are over four hundred thousand women lawyers,
making up almost 36 percent of all the practicing attorneys in the US.
Despite several fits and starts, both legal and cultural, to move women
up through the ranks of law firms, even today, "women are 29 percent

less likely to reach the first level of partnership than men," according to McKinsey & Company's inaugural Women in Law Firms study. This is a serious challenge, since over half the students in law school are women.

What's worse is that private law firms have held on tight to their well-established cultural norms of male leadership. The Law360 Glass Ceiling report for 2019 cited the lack of progress at the top levels of law firms for women. Their report sounded like another LeanIn.org obituary on the inability of women to enter the leadership of these firms. At the top private law firms, four-fifths of equity partners are men—which means that only 20 percent are women.

It doesn't have to be that way, however, and women are entering the top ranks of law firms, albeit slowly. Andie Kramer is one woman whose story inspired me because she hasn't just become a partner and a leader; she is also helping other women break through the gender bias. She is working hard to change the systems, attitudes, practices, values, and beliefs of these firms' cultures so women can feel they matter and belong. Andie is a testament that women can thrive in their legal careers and smash any myths holding them back.

Andie Kramer was in grade school when she went with her social studies class to a criminal court building on the South Side of Chicago. She watched as an attorney defended a poor young man who seemed to be innocent of the murder for which he was eventually convicted. She was so moved, inspired, and activated by the experience that she came home and told her parents that she was going to be an attorney—and save the world.

Her parents had one friend who was an attorney, and they asked him to meet with her for lunch and give her the facts about what it was really like to be a lawyer. Andie met with him, thinking he was going to help her become what she envisioned. Instead, for the entire lunch he told her why she should not want to be a lawyer; that no one liked lady lawyers; that no one would ever be her friend; that she would be lonely; and she would never get married or have a family. If she did become a lawyer, no one would want to talk to her, and she would live her life alone.

Andie was outraged. Little did her parents' friend realize that his career counseling would boomerang. Andie took his challenge and became a highly successful attorney, a partner in a prestigious firm, an author of four books, an editor of two other books, and a well-known leader, advocating for women in every profession.

Let's look at the cultural stories, those myths that Andie's parents' friend was proselytizing and why they continue to hold women back from integrating with and leading law firms forward. As we do, I encourage you to consider the following as you read on: What can women bring to the table? What barriers are at the gate? And why are men so resistant to letting them in?

The Myth

Where did this all come from, a myth that women will not be good lawyers and will certainly not be happy ones? Cynthia Grant Bowman has a wonderful history of women in the legal profession that begins with her story of Jane Foster, a 1918 graduate of Cornell Law School. Although Foster had graduated near the top of her class, had become an editor of the *Cornell Law Quarterly*, and been elected to the Order of the Coif, she could not get a job in a law firm as a lawyer. Through a faculty referral she managed to become a legal assistant in the New York City firm of Davies, Auerbach, and Cornell, where she worked from 1918 to 1929. She watched the men make partner, while there was no place for her to go. She tried to get a position at White & Case, a Wall Street firm. They wrote to the Cornell Law School's dean, saying that despite Jane's exceptional experience and strong recommendations, "Here in this office we have steadfastly refused to take women on our legal staff, and I know we will continue to adhere to that policy."

Foster eventually dropped out of law altogether. She had invested smartly and held stock in the company that was to become IBM. She focused her skills in law and business to assist her friends and the Cornell Law School, amassing a fortune. In 1989, Cornell dedicated the Jane Foster addition to Myron Taylor Hall.

Jane's life was not unlike that of most women in the nineteenth and twentieth centuries who aspired to become successful attorneys. There is a long history of keeping women out of law firms, and then, even when they managed to gain entry, they were kept out of partnerships, which still holds true in many firms across the country. Women were getting into law schools, including the most prestigious, doing extremely well, and then finding themselves unwanted in law firms of virtually any size, from the large Wall Street firms to smaller-sized firms.

For most of the twentieth century it was difficult, if not impossible, for women to smash through the barriers in the legal profession. Only a small number of women achieved positions of influence. We must not forget how Ruth Bader Ginsburg, a Supreme Court Justice, graduated from Columbia University Law School in 1959 first in her class. She sent out letters and resumes to a large number of New York firms and was ignored or rejected by every one of them. And former Supreme Court Justice Sandra Day O'Connor, close to the top of her class at Stanford in 1952, only managed to get offered a legal secretary position. In fact, many law firms were rather proud of the fact that they protected their old-boy network and had perhaps one or two women at their firms, quotas filled primarily by entry-level positions.

The entire system was rife with walls preventing women from moving past the degree stage. Even at their law schools, the placement offices told them they would never get a job in a Wall Street firm and certainly not in any firm that might lead to a partner position. Those few women who managed to gain positions in these firms usually found themselves unsuccessful at trying to attend meetings and lunches in an all-men's club. Women were well aware not to ask for favors and knew that if they needed maternity leave, they might not be able to return to their jobs.

Despite the fact that 36 percent of attorneys today are women, and over 50 percent of law school students are women, the working environments have been slow to include them, build cultures that embrace their styles and tones, and essentially change. Instead, the cultures remain stuck in their male-dominated, traditional view of the world where women are—

- **Discriminated against.** In the 2015 gender-bias survey conducted by the National Association for Law Placement (NALP), only 17.4 percent of women were equity partners in the surveyed US law firms. There were 28.8 percent women working as non-equity partners.

- **Stereotyped.** Traditional gender stereotypes seem to have a hard time dying. Male attorneys still assume that a female attorney is too soft to manage an aggressive negotiation and incapable of managing a complex litigation. On the other hand, women who act outside of traditional stereotypes and show they can handle difficult legal projects face negative backlash and isolation.

- **Not allowed to have work-life balance.** This remains one area where little progress has been made. Lawyers work late hours and must be accessible 24/7. Firms are not particularly sensitive to the needs of mothers, and single mothers have an especially difficult time balancing the demands of their home life and their workloads. The hope is that technology will enable women to have flexible hours and the ability to work virtually from their homes or elsewhere.

- **Facing sexual harassment.** While lawyers preach to their clients that they must temper their workplace harassment, women still find themselves facing harassment on the job. Whether it is the long hours, the frequent travel, or their autonomy, their workplace cultures have not been able to eliminate unwelcome advances. Requests for sexual favors, verbal or physical advances, and the continued use of gender issues to intimidate in trial situations persists. While trending downward, one-third of the women in the legal profession still report these issues.

- **Paid less than men.** The persistence of the gender–wage gap is frustrating in every profession. You might think that in an industry built on laws, women would earn the same as men. In 2015, however, Bureau of Labor Statistics data shows that the gender wage gap is as high as 40 percent in the legal profession, with women earning 60 cents for every dollar earned by a man. The myth is that the men pull in more business and work more hours. In fact, that is not the case. Women continue to make less even when they pull in more business and often work more hours than their male counterparts.

Which brings us to Andie Kramer and the personal and professional world she has created. When I read about all the women who tried and failed to succeed in the legal profession, I had to wonder what Andie Kramer's life was like and how she beat the odds. After speaking with her, I learned it was a combination of destiny, luck, smarts, and personality. Here's her story.

Meet Andie Kramer

In 1972, Andie headed off to the University of Illinois at Urbana-Champaign for her undergraduate degree and then on to Northwestern for her law degree, graduating in 1978 with honors and distinction at each institution. While in law school, she thought she was on her way to a successful career. During the summer between her second and third year of law school, she got a summer job with the expectation that it would land her a permanent job after she graduated. Andie recalls that it was a great summer job with a large firm and was, what she thought, a perfectly wonderful experience to set her up for the future. She even received notes from the partners with all types of praise and compliments. One said, "This is amazing. You can't really be a summer lawyer. You're a real lawyer in disguise."

As the summer internship ended, she expected to get her offer. Instead, the head of the summer program called to tell her she did not have an offer. She was dumbfounded. She had a wall full of praise and had performed like a rock star. When she asked why she was not being offered a position, he told her that one of the senior partners had said she would get a job "over his dead body!"

Afterward, Andie reflected on what had happened and what she had misunderstood. During her internship she had been called into that partner's spacious office, and as Andie shared with me, "I only talked to him for fifteen minutes. What could have possibly gone wrong? As I worked my way through what had happened, I remembered that I was called into his office by his assistant. As I got to his office, he was sitting at his desk with his feet propped up and his hands behind his head in a classic power pose. It was clear that he was telling me that he was important, and I was certainly not. Because I go by Andie and not Andrea, he was surprised to see a woman enter his office that day. He probably thought his summer interns were all guys: Fred, Bob, and Andy."

She continued, "He looked at me and had no sense of who I was or why I was standing at his door. I walked in and introduced myself. I had always been told that you shake hands with somebody when you meet them the first time. No one had told me that if a man, a partner no less, is sitting with his feet on the desk with his hands behind his head, you are going to play a power game with him if you try and shake his hand. He would have to stand up to shake yours, which he did in my case. So I walked toward his desk and extended my hand. It was a bad move. He motioned me over to a low couch that looked like a dog bed. I noticed he had two guest chairs by his desk. I remember thinking that I was *not* going to sit on that dog bed. I sat on one of his guest chairs instead. The conversation pretty much went downhill from there. He decided right then and there that I was an uppity 'bitch,' and over *his* dead body would I get a job at his law firm. I learned the hard way that the gender dance was just beginning and how I danced my part really mattered if I was going to thrive as an attorney."

At the time, Andie thought her career as an attorney was over before it had even begun. Instead, this rather sobering experience set her on a different path that has shaped her life and her career. After graduation, she received offers from some of the biggest law firms in the country but chose instead to go to a law firm that had seven lawyers. This small, growing firm, at the time called Coffield, Ungaretti, Harris & Slavin, needed a tax lawyer. She was going to start the tax department, right out of school. As she reflects on that position today, she realizes it was quite bold for them and for her. They were going to hire a tax expert to support her, as needed. The firm would arrange for training. It was a perfect opportunity for Andie to build something, for herself and for the firm, and it gave her a very different perspective on the world she was moving into.

At this firm, Andie was treated as if she were a full contributing member of the organization without any regard to the fact that she was a woman. As Andie told me, "They couldn't care less if lawyers were purple polka-dotted. If they did a good job, everyone wanted them on their projects." It was the perfect environment for Andie to develop as a tax attorney and as a successful woman in business.

And that is where she met her husband, Alton Harris. Al and Andie worked closely together, building his law firm and their own careers. Andie had their daughter in 1990 and began to evaluate her own career options. With a baby in tow and a career in bloom, Andie left the firm in 1993 to go to McDermott Will & Emery LLP, a large firm where she came head-on to a totally different cultural reality. At McDermott, the stereotypes and biases against women were everywhere. On the one hand, she was new, and she was a woman with a young child. The men quickly boxed her in. As a woman, they didn't think she should have her own clients or a fancy corner office. They were puzzled as to why she was even there. Things got pretty nasty. She was trying to build her practice, and she had a two-year-old daughter at home. She met resistance every step of the way.

One of the partners asked her to move to their New York office because her practice was sort of a New York capital markets practice; he told her that she could go home on weekends. But Andie countered, telling him, "If I wanted to go to a New York firm, I would have done that, and I have a two-year-old at home." She stood her ground and stayed put, adding, "I'm a mother, and the stereotypes about mothers are that we are totally incompetent and only care about our families. So I knew what he was doing when he would start calling me for the one project that I did with him, asking me, 'Will you be available to speak to me? I'd like to talk to you at 5:00 p.m., if you'll still be around.' So I intentionally never made myself available at 5:00. I could have been doing nothing, but there was no way I was going to meet him. I offered to meet him instead at 6:00 or at 6:30 or at 7:00 or at 8:00 that night. And he never took me up on that. I offered to meet him any time after 6:00 the next morning, and he was never a taker for that either."

Some people would wonder why Andie was being defiant. Actually, I understand clearly what she was trying to do—get men to adapt to, respect, and include women on their terms. Yet each time she offered an alternate time to meet, he said he was unavailable. Why were he and others unwilling to bend yet expecting her to accommodate them?

Meanwhile, Andie continued to move up in the firm. She was elected to the management committee and then served a three-year term on the compensation committee. As unusual as it was for a woman to be on those committees, Andie used the experiences to develop a different perspective on professional services organizations and the men running them. What she found was that women and men tend to communicate differently, and it matters greatly how the messages are heard and how the responses are crafted. Men see women as less ambitious, less competent, and less able to handle complex cases. Women, on the other hand, are socialized to worry more about how the other person feels. They may in fact feel more pressure about getting people aligned around goals and collaborative solutions at the expense of getting ahead themselves. Women tend to undermine their own capabilities by saying things like, "I'm sorry, this might be a dumb idea, but ..." or "I don't know if I missed something important, but I'm thinking this ..."

When speaking like this, women send the message that they don't know what they are talking about, while undermining their own authority and confidence. Andie found this come through so clearly when she served on the compensation committee. She read every self-evaluation and every review that a senior lawyer submitted about a junior lawyer. What she learned was that the world seemed to fall into two buckets. The men would write self-evaluations about how they had single-handedly scaled the Empire State Building (metaphorically, of course). They had rescued eighteen damsels in distress. And they had saved the client half a billion dollars. The guys were all rock stars and deserved everything.

On the other hand, the women would write in their self-evaluations about how they were on a specific team and had worked with others to save the client a lot of money. Consequently, when it came time for bonuses and promotions, the men were rewarded, and the women were left wondering what had happened to them.

This prompted Andie to write "Bragging Rights: Self-Evaluation Dos and Don'ts."

This radicalized Andie, in a good way. She began to write about the self-evaluation process, the dos and don'ts and what a woman should say about herself and how to communicate her achievements. Then she began to speak about it. She is the author of many articles on gender communications and coauthor on the American Bar Association guide *What Women Need to Know about Negotiating Compensation*. She cowrote a book with her husband titled *Breaking Through Bias: Communication Techniques for Women to Succeed at Work*.

Breaking Through Bias is about how the gender stereotypes of cultures—men, women, work, families, leadership, and community—become a common way in which we order our lives. But they also hold women back. Women start their careers on parity with men but in general end them far earlier and too often before they have achieved commensurate success, compensation, and inclusion. Andie's approach is to offer an integrated set of communication techniques designed for women in whatever setting they are in. Tailored for women in male-dominated business settings, the techniques show women how to anticipate gender bias and avoid or overcome negative gender stereotypes.

What Andie learned in her management committee meetings was that women have to manage the impressions they create among men. Andie and her husband call this "the Goldilocks Dilemma," because women face a double bind where they are seen as weak and incompetent if they are nice, but seen as competent and unpleasant to work with if they display traditionally male behaviors. Because of this dilemma, women's behaviors are rarely considered to be just right. To address this, they must communicate in a way that doesn't deny who they are. This competent but likable role is more balanced and accepted by their male counterparts. Andie's hope is to pay it forward and share her experiences with other women so they can break through gender bias in the workplace and reach the career success they desire and deserve.

Her first book led Andie and Al to do more research that turned into their next book, *It's Not You, It's the Workplace: Women's Conflict at Work and the Bias that Built It.* Al and Andie realized they were on a mission to change the myths that were keeping women in their proverbial place and allowing men to benefit at women's expense. After the first book's success, their speaking engagements expanded, and they realized that women's interpersonal relationships with other women at work were far more complicated than they first believed. What they kept hearing were stories from women about other women who were difficult to work with, unpleasant to be around, and referred to as back-stabbing bitches. This piqued their curiosity, and they wondered if women were their own worst enemies. Were they that difficult to work with?

What they found was that this was hardly true. But it was a strong part of the cultural mythology and difficult to upend. One telling story came from a woman who told Andie, "You don't talk about women working with women. I get along fine with the men. I hate working with women." When asked to describe this more fully, the woman told her that she hated working with the women so much that she had gone to her boss about them. He told her to just work with the men.

When Andie asked, "How did the women you worked for treat you differently from the way the men treated you?" The woman fell silent and started to cry and said, "They treated me exactly the same as the men did, and I trashed them and their careers." She had been holding women to a different standard and had needs they weren't fulfilling for her. The men were getting the job done but little else. This woman wanted something more from her female colleagues. She wanted a mother or a big sister, or a deeper friend, and was lost and upset that they didn't provide her with the kindness, handholding, and caring she was expecting from them.

This cultural phenomenon led Al and Andie to begin their social science research. They needed to know why women had these problems with interpersonal relationships with other women. After interviews with hundreds of women and a deep dive into the academic social science research, they concluded that these stereotypes and biases in the brains drove women and men to feel and act in certain ways toward each other. The issue was the masculine cultures, values, and traditions of most workplaces that have created the gendered workplace. The confirmation biases were so strong, in fact, that they overrode the factual reality.

When speaking with Andie, the woman also shared that women have problems with other women in the workplace not because they are harder to work with but because they expect them to work according to their stereotype. They want other women to be nice and kind, like "women are supposed to be." We get angry with them because they are acting like a boss—like a guy might. We create these environments that force women, when there's one seat at the table, to be in competition with each other in a way that men never have to experience and don't understand.

Andie has taken her passion for changing the workplace cultures and enabling women to have a fair chance to climb into the leadership of law firms. She created the gender diversity committee at McDermott, which in turn resulted in a committee for LGBTQ lawyers in the firm. Over the years her firm leaders have worked hard to change the gendered nature of their workplace and to acknowledge the stereotypes, biases, and behaviors that affect their interpersonal relationships on all levels. While she no longer heads the committee, she did find ways to make the environment less toxic for a diverse community.

As that evolved, Andie launched the Women's Leadership and Mentoring Alliance with two other women. The alliance has developed mentorship programs to help other women. One lesson Andie learned through all of her research, work, and writing is that women are searching for a sisterhood. The trick is that the workplace sisterhood requires women to navigate the political dynamics of the workplace, making it different from those close-knit friendships that they might have outside of work. A workplace sisterhood does not require women to become best friends. It asks them to work together for the common good of all women.

As Andie overcame the walls, hurdles, and ceilings set before her, she realized that women, attorneys, her female clients, and others are searching for something more than proving they are smart and capable. They are people who need and want to belong to groups of others who share similar values, beliefs, conversations, behaviors, and, most of all, those central stories. Andie was able to become successful through her stories. Through their stories, people know themselves and how their lives become meaningful. These women are on a search for a place where they can belong, either a tribe or a clan or simply a great place to work where they can find meaning.

From the Observation Deck

Even though we think of law firms as professional services firms, they are fundamentally businesses, first and foremost. They have to attract talented people who have the skills clients demand and that colleagues need to collaborate and communicate effectively. It might sound rather obvious, but, like every business, law firms need a healthy balance sheet and income statement. They must have a high-quality product delivered with exceptional service. Further, for a firm to succeed, they need men and women who know how to develop and operate a business.

But it is a great deal more than just that. The quality of the firm is often a direct reflection of the culture created and lived by men and women who are there to serve a diversity of clients. What Andie's story showed so clearly is that a law firm demands a corporate culture in which ideas thrive and diversity is lived, not just preached. And, as Andie will tell you, if a corporate culture is not designed and built with intentionality, people create one of their own that fits their values, beliefs, and styles.

As firms build their businesses, these issues of diversity and inclusion are critically important. It is more than fairness. Research demonstrates that firms that have diverse thinking come up with better solutions. When people surround themselves with others like them, the affinity bias takes over, and people flock to others where they feel most comfortable. Without cognitive diversity in the mix, the leadership might not even know what they are missing. Those firms that tap into a culture of true inclusion are more profitable and provide better client results.

Andie's story tells us a great deal about American society. Her story is all about male-female relationships and the sacred traditions in the legal profession that men want to secure. In some ways, women are pressuring the very essence of who those men are and the world they believe to be true. Yet much is happening that offers hope, particularly now that the number of women in law school exceeds 50 percent of the class.

The pressure is coming from outside, from those female clients and others, and from the women inside, to transform these firms. With 40 percent of businesses in the US now owned by women, the clients of law firms are asking for a different type of relationship with their attorneys. Often women business owners want a legal team that includes women. These business owners, in turn, are driving some of these changes faster than the men realize or want to accept.

We also have women who are leaving and opening up their own practices, quickly picking up clients and building prestigious businesses that work for them, their partners, and their clients. One, for example, left a large firm where she was doing quite well but where she wasn't sure she was fulfilling her purpose and passions. Instead, she launched her own firm, when she realized she had a wonderful network that was willing to refer great clients to her. She hired attorneys who wanted a different work style and built a great firm. She hired talented women, some of whom were coming back from raising their children. Rather than telling them how many hours they had to work, she asked them what they would like to earn and how many hours that might involve. She also went virtual, using technology to support remote talent, and she has attracted quality talent to support her growing business.

Not all women want to run their own business, however. Women must continue to push law firms to rethink their cultures and transform the myths holding those affinity biases, gender biases, and confirmation biases in place. From what I have seen, many companies have a narrow picture of their cultures and are quick to blame and complain about the problem, often pointing the finger at women. To address this, companies should mentor and coach their employees on how to build better relationships with each other and recognize the value their female employees have to offer the company, placing them in the more senior roles traditionally reserved for men. To help organizations overcome gender bias, Andie and Al developed a seven-step program set out in their book *It's Not You, It's the Workplace*. The program is well-designed to help organizations change their policies and procedures to remove bias from career-affecting decisions.

As I look at recent trends, I am seeing that change is happening slowly in this once-resistant industry. The larger law firms are beginning to expand the number of partners who are women or people of diverse backgrounds. In December of 2018, the percentage of women partners in the top fifteen firms ranged from 21 percent to 53 percent. Overall, 38 percent of *new* equity and nonequity partners in the top fifteen firms were women. African Americans (both men and women) and Latino and Asian women were a very small percentage (2 percent) of those rising into the partner ranks.

For men who are lawyers, viewing women as fitting into their own story means their story has to change. Changing stories among adults means working hard on the plasticity of the brain to see things through a new lens. When I work with people or organizations, I have them visualize a new way of doing things that they can embrace. Then I have them develop small wins, almost as practice sessions, to test the new way of doing things to see how it evolves into a new story about them. They are always the heroes of their stories. But they need new behaviors to support these new beliefs. None of this is easy. But all of it is essential if women are going to become part of a new culture inside and outside of these firms.

Change is fundamentally challenging. The men's club is resisting the changes because they feel vulnerable. Getting them to change the game and see women as allies instead of enemies, creating better places for them to work, will not be easy. But slowly, the changes are coming. As one attorney said to me, even the men are beginning to take paternity leave and spend three months with their newborn child, without getting penalized for their life choice in their firms. Thank goodness for those millennials who are going to help change our culture in purposeful ways. And thank goodness for Andie Kramer and Al Harris, who continue to push the rock up the hill so others may have an easier climb.

Women Cannot Manage Money

"A woman's best protection is a little money of her own."

—*Clare Boothe Luce, American author
and US Ambassador*

I met Janine Firpo through my editor, who said, "You should include Janine in your book. She is trying to change the way women are managing their money all across the globe." Janine is, indeed, on her way to making women far better at thinking about money, understanding how to invest in building their resources, and finding a community of other women who share similar beliefs and values. Janine had to face some significant obstacles on her road to financial comfort and investment expertise. The challenges she overcame and the path she followed has led her to exceptional leadership roles with personal growth and societal impact.

She has a great story to share. The myths she was confronting are the same for women everywhere. The recurring mythology is that women cannot manage their money; they are averse to risking their money and haven't a clue how to invest it wisely, but they sure can spend it. So men have to take charge of the household finances, dole out a woman's weekly allowance, and care for any inheritance she might have acquired. These myths drove behavior in the not-so-distant past and continue for some women even today. To gain a richer perspective, we need to step back and look at the changes taking place in how women are earning their livings and investing their money. Could a little anthropology create a fresh lens to see why we believe things to be the way they are or were? If we continue to think that women are incapable of managing their finances, we remain lost in a sea of stories confirming these myths, often propagated by the very people who can capitalize on them.

Today, there is far more hope to the story that goes well beyond gender limitations and cultural biases. These changes are redefining the next phase in our evolution, a truly transformative one. They are helping us rethink how to raise our daughters. For our next generation to smash this myth, we must change how we raise our children to earn and manage their financial resources.

The Myth

In the 1970s I was recently out of college, married, and ready for a credit card of my own. I was a graduate student, was working, had no children, and was married. There was no way that I, as a woman, could have easily gotten a credit card. Back then, women could not have a bank credit card unless they had their husband's signature—even if you were a famous tennis star, as was the case with three-time Wimbledon champion Billie Jean King.

By the 1970s, 43 percent of the labor force was occupied by women. However, it took an act of Congress in 1974 to finally change the rules allowing women to get loans, credit cards, and even home mortgages without a man signing on their loan, when they passed the Equal Credit Opportunity Act to ban sex discrimination in lending. By 1980, single women bought one-third of all condominiums and one-tenth of all homes. Today, I know several well-employed women who have purchased homes. They have invited their male significant others to share them, as long as they have a job and pay part of the expenses.

If you are a woman today, you might be paying off your college debt or your credit cards. As you read this, you might wonder why women were not allowed to take out a credit card or a car loan until the last forty years. And perhaps you are wondering why it is so much easier today. Were women that different then? Or was it more that our society, conceived and managed by men, was happier taking charge of women, their money, and their lives?

The myth, developed over hundreds of years in many different cultures, was that women were unable to manage money. Men, fathers, husbands, or financial institutions had to dole out an allowance each week for a woman's household needs to protect her from the "misfortunes" of easy credit. Women were considered vulnerable. However, they were quite capable of earning a living. They undoubtedly worked in the agricultural fields of the early settlers, entered the workforce to help during each of the world wars, and continue to thrive in the workforce today in many industries, from sweatshops to factories to accounting and engineering firms.

But back then women were more like property than free members of society. Remember that in 1769, following English law, the colonies created their law where women became the property of men after marriage. All of a woman's inheritance, wealth, or personal money was owned and controlled by men, for the presumed protection of their wives. It wasn't until 1844 that a married woman in Maine became the first in the US to win the right to own her property. Four years later New York passed the Married Woman's Property Act. But it wasn't until 1900 that other states passed their own laws to support women's rights to own and manage their own property.

The question until the late twentieth century was: Were women incapable of managing money, even if they were capable of earning it? Or was this myth simply a way for men and society to control women? Meanwhile, a growing body of research continues to force us to rethink the foundation of these myths. Tahira Hira, Iowa State

University professor of consumer economics, and Cäzilia Loibl, an assistant professor at the Department of Consumer Sciences at The Ohio State University, studied 911 randomly selected US households with annual household incomes of $75,000 or higher. Their report, titled *Gender Differences in Investment Behavior*, was published in 2006 and funded by the NASD Investor Education Foundation. This gender study suggested that there were some differences, albeit small, between men and women. The differences seemed to reflect their different roles in the labor market, their salaries, and what they did in their homes. The research was quite crucial in terms of what they found women doing and how women saw themselves. What the research found was that women were in charge of how money was spent every day, and both men and women saved and invested every month at almost the same levels. There was almost no difference. There was a different level in confidence, with only about 50 percent of the women describing themselves as confident or knowledgeable about investing. Once educated, they do as well as or even better than men. So why the illusion that women could not manage their money and had to have their spouses dole it out to them?

As Helaine Olen reminds us in her book *Pound Foolish: Exposing the Dark Side of the Personal Finance Industry*, "I think that myth persists because women themselves believe it. It's the old joke: Men think they're the expert if they just say something about something. Women have a PhD in a topic, and they're still concerned they don't really know enough," she explains, and "that's a large part of it." In Janine's story, you will learn how she is working to smash that myth and to empower other women to be stewards of their own wealth.

Meet Janine Firpo

Janine has been on a lifelong mission to change the way women earn, manage, and invest their money. She sees herself as part of an emerging community of successful women who do things differently and want others to have the opportunities to do the same.

Her story is an important one. It shows us how we might have to change the way we raise our children. Of particular importance is how we teach girls and boys how to think about and manage money. Parental and societal attitudes must create a new set of cultural values, beliefs, and behaviors for the future—a new culture and the myths that support it where women are capable of earning and investing their earnings. Men don't have to care for them. They just need the knowledge and support to make the right investment decisions.

Much of Janine's own beliefs and her lifelong behaviors developed while she was growing up. Reflecting on her childhood, Janine shared that she had impoverished parents. Janine's parents were Depression-era kids. Her mother lived throughout her life with a poverty mindset and had to work hard to support herself and her family. She ultimately became the primary breadwinner in the house. Her dad was a native San Franciscan who grew up in an area called Potrero Hill. It was known as Goat Hill, because many people there raised goats. At that time, Janine's family had pigeons they raised for food. Her dad, the son of Italian immigrants, was, as she said, "super poor." He was lucky if he would get an orange for Christmas, and the dumps were his playground.

Janine's mom was the daughter of Hungarian immigrants. Her mother's parents emigrated to Bethlehem, Pennsylvania, and started a farm there. When her mom was quite young, Janine's grandfather died tragically, from falling onto one of the pieces of farm equipment. The only way her grandmother could manage was to send her mother's older brother off on his own when he was only fifteen. Her grandmother then moved to New York, where she had relatives. She became a "sometimes live-in" housemaid and had to put her other two children into a boarding school.

The issue of money for Janine's parents—for Janine's mother, in particular—became an overriding focus in their life. Her mother never went to college. She didn't have enough money. Yet Janine remembers her as being resourceful and smart. At eighteen, her mother got out of the boarding school to become a secretary. She was doing well financially and decided to move across the country from New York to San Francisco. There she met Janine's dad, a former bomber pilot in the Second World War, and they married. At the time he was in law school, but six months later he dropped out because law school did not suit him, and he found a position in sales. That was not a great fit for his personality either. Janine's mother, realizing that she was moving, once again, into a struggle for her daily money, went back to work. Those early years, when Janine and her sisters were starting out in life, were lean. They wore hand-me-down clothes, scrimped, and often worried if there would be enough money for food.

Now, I am not suggesting that for a woman to learn how to manage money, she should grow up without any. And neither is Janine. Her mother became a role model who showed her how women could hurdle the obstacles they often face and seize control of their destiny. There was a time when Janine's mother reached a breaking point. As Janine remembers her mother: "She really reminds me of that scene in *Gone with the Wind*, where she stands in the field and says, 'I swear I will never be hungry again.'"

Her mother got a job as a secretary at Hewlett-Packard and then realized she needed to do more. She figured out that real estate was the area for her. And she eventually built a successful residential real estate business in Foster City, a suburb of San Francisco. Not only did she work as a real estate sales woman; she also bought her own properties. When Janine was young, her mother would go to the court steps to buy foreclosures. During the summers, Janine and her sisters would help their mom fix up these properties so they could rent or resell them.

At first, Janine's dad did not trust what her mother was doing. Her mother was driving the purchase of real estate and managing their stock investments. He was far more risk-averse than she was. As he saw her make money for them, he came to realize that she knew what she was doing and let her handle things on her own.

While her mother eventually did well, she never forgot the lessons she learned from being poor. As Janine remembers, "This is a woman who, when I was a kid, would drive across town with coupons to save five cents on something. Even into her eighties and nineties, she would still write letters rather than pay for a cross-country phone call. She just never lost that sense of frugalness. As a kid, there was a lot of talk about money, money, money, and how to save and make money. It was just a deep-seated fear with my mom."

As they got older, Janine's mother insisted on teaching her daughters what she had learned. Her training came out of a necessity that she never wanted for them. She made them start saving money when they were tiny. She helped them understand budgeting, drawing them into her money situation. They knew when she was doing well and when she wasn't. Janine's mother showed them how the real estate market worked. They were aware when she was having trouble with a tenant and how she had to make it all work out. She knew that only through these experiences could they become skilled at managing their own assets in the future.

As time went on, Janine learned how to think about money, how to earn it, and how to invest it. Her training continued when Janine's mother started investing in the stock market. In the 1980s, the wisdom was "to buy blue-chip companies and hold them for the future." That strategy served Janine's mother well.

Her mother also helped Janine with the down payment on the first houses that she bought. As Janine recalls, "My mom went with me to look for houses—the first two houses I bought—to teach me how naïve I was about some of the choices I wanted to make. She wasn't always kind with the way that she would train me, but she was training me, nevertheless. While I might not have appreciated it that much then, I sure do now!"

Janine's mother figured out that she should set up trusts so she could avoid probate and help her daughters more easily manage her estate after her death. Wanting to mitigate her tax implications as much as possible, she did everything legally possible to shelter her properties and reduce her tax burdens. She was also adamant that her daughters share equally and appropriately in her legacy. There was never a question in anyone's minds of one sister trying to get more than the others or thinking they would get more than the others. As Janine's mother got older, she continued to share all of her wisdom about the nuances of money.

What is equally impressive is how Janine wasn't shielded from her mother's financial life but intimately included in it. It was a shared journey. Reflecting on her adolescent years, Janine remembers that "when it comes to money, I think that's a big Achilles heel that a lot of women have. Money is still taboo. It's hidden. We don't talk about it. We're afraid of it. But whenever you shine a light on something that you fear, the fear begins to go away. I think it's essential to shine a light on money, and I think that it was incredibly important for me."

Her mother's lessons framed Janine's story. It became a core part of who she is and how she sees the world. Three driving forces shaped Janine's life. The first was never to be financially needy and never to be dependent on a man for money or the things she wanted. Second, she had to find something intellectually stimulating, as well as on the leading edge of what was happening. And third was the importance of having a purpose. Though none of these were evident at the beginning of her journey, all emerged out of her core values and beliefs. She had a willingness to step out beyond the cultural norms of how a woman should behave and belong.

Janine's journey is an important one for others. It was never a straight line like people expect of a successful woman. She had to find her way through a maze of lifelong adventures. For example, Janine thought she wanted to be a doctor. However, she realized that it was not her passion, so it wasn't the road she wanted to pursue. Studying marine biology in Florida was her next idea, but that meant Janine would be spending a lot of time underwater helping others do research, which was not her thing either. Then someone mentioned that computer technology might be a hot area to consider, and not knowing much about it, she leaped into the sector early on. The 1980s were remarkable in the infancy of what is, today, so ubiquitous when it comes to technology. For Janine, it was either a lucky move or a brilliant one that set the stage for the rest of her journey.

Janine headed back to San Francisco to work in the high-tech sector, doing well financially. She saved her money, and before she turned thirty, she had bought her first house. It was the beginning of her effort to be self-sufficient. As she thinks about herself, "I was very frugal and had bag lady syndrome. I believed one day I would be old and eating cat food under the bridge." That was not what she wanted, so she worked hard to have a different future.

Starting her career in 1981 as an assembly language programmer, Janine quickly advanced through a series of positions, including roles at Apple and several high-tech start-ups. After fifteen years in the high-tech industry, she quit her job as vice president of a start-up and took a four-month backpacking trip through sub-Saharan Africa. When she left on that trip, everyone she knew was in the CD-ROM industry. However, when she returned, the multimedia industry had flipped to the internet. She knows it sounds strange that in only four months such a dramatic change had taken place. Janine saw the future was coming in a far different format. While she could have jumped into the emergent internet industry, her purpose had changed.

After seeing the incredible poverty all across Africa, Janine wanted to find a way to work at the intersection of technology and business to solve the significant social development problems she had seen. Despite the internet boom and some of her previous colleagues becoming billionaires, her role was to find a way to share what she had learned on a bigger stage.

She went to Washington, DC, and networked with all types of agencies, picking up work with a woman who was a consultant to USAID and building technology infrastructure in Africa. This woman needed more people to help her. She realized that Janine had the technical knowledge and had traveled around Africa by herself, proving that she wouldn't freak out when she worked there. Many technologists at the time had the technical knowledge but were unable to adjust to the realities in Africa. This dual capability became Janine's trademark, launching her into a new career that blossomed from there.

After a period of working in DC, Janine was recruited to Hewlett-Packard when CEO Carly Fiorina was there. Carly Fiorina had an idea. Could the company find growth by building technology solutions for poor people in emerging nations? Janine was asked to join a group of, as she called them, "primarily white men and women," none of whom had ever been to Africa. Their job was to figure out how HP could make technology work for the poor, even though they had no direct experience with these eventual customers or the realities of their lives. Because HP was a leading provider to the financial services industry, the company wanted to determine if there was a role for them in bringing financial services to the poor. Janine was asked to go figure that out, leading her to learn about microfinance and the possibility of scaling that business fifteen times beyond what it was then.

Janine and her team started exploring point-of-sale devices in Uganda in 2004. Meanwhile, other firms were experimenting in this arena as well. Vodacom was playing around with cell phones in Kenya, and that hit pay dirt. While it took three years, Vodacom ultimately developed a mobile phone service called M-Pesa, which became an amazingly successful mechanism for moving money around Kenya. Launched in 2007, M-Pesa helped spawn an entire new industry referred to as mobile money. Janine shifted her focus and became one of the earliest mobile money experts.

Over the next ten years, Janine took her expertise in financial services, e-payments, and mobile banking and provided strategic implementation support to mobile operators, financial institutions, and technology companies. They shared her belief in delivering new business solutions to emerging markets. In 2012, she joined the Bill & Melinda Gates Foundation as a deputy director in financial services for the poor. Her team was skilled at helping poor people emerge from poverty and enter the formal economy. She helped design philanthropic and impact investments that took big ideas and helped them work.

Before joining the foundation, Janine worked with the International Finance Corporation, a subsidiary of the World Bank. She also held the role of president and founder of Sevak Solutions, a nonprofit company that she spun out of her work at HP before Carly Fiorina left the company. Sevak Solutions was involved in technology prototyping and consulting services related to financial services to the poor.

At this point, Janine retired from her career because the work was becoming boring to her. The stuff that she loved was no longer part of what people were doing. For Janine, when mobile money became big business, it lost its cutting edge. She started thinking about what she wanted to do next so that she could continue to grow and learn new things. She thrives whenever she is pushing the envelope. If she isn't pushing forward, then, as she says, "What's the point?"

As she reflected on what matters to her now, and perhaps always has been her driving force, she shared her vision: "I have always wanted to play much bigger. I used to talk about moving mountains. And I want to move mountains. An old boyfriend of mine said to me once, 'You know, Janine, even if you move a mountain, you probably won't notice, because it's so big and you probably won't know that you moved it a little bit.' And I said, I don't care. I don't need to know at the end of the day that I actually moved the mountain, but that's the goal."

Janine has been tracking the social entrepreneur and impact-investing spheres for at least twenty years. She has committed to moving all of her investments into asset classes, funds, and private placements that align with her values. As such, she is a member of the Seattle Impact Investors Group, and sits on the board of Zebras Unite, a movement to develop alternative forms of start-up capital and support. Janine has served on the boards of what is now the Presidio Graduate School and Water.org. She was also an early advisor to Kiva.org.

Janine is part of a group of women who have created a new approach to angel investing, called the Next Wave Impact Fund. NWIF's job is to help increase women's participation investing in start-up businesses that align with their social and personal values. The fund is designed to help women learn by doing while also working to increase diversity, inclusion, and impact. Their focus is on early-stage investing and entrepreneurial ecosystems. Their global fund has ninety-nine women investors, twenty-five of whom are women of color. Janine is a member of the experienced ten-woman investment committee. NWIF brings these women investors together to build a diversified portfolio of socially relevant investments. These investments and the companies they are supporting all have social purposes. Focused on sustainability and environmental impact, these companies also must still have profitable financial returns.

Janine's vision is to engage with women and educate them. She is working with others to develop a multimedia approach where women will learn through written materials, podcasts, webinars, and workshops. From her experience and expertise gained in developing countries, Janine wants to continue to rethink how women develop the skills and confidence to invest their monies. As she shared with me, it is time for women to be able to do what they want to do—namely, help society—as well as invest in those ideas and businesses that can have an impact on society.

Janine is currently working on a book that can become the tool kit women can use to build their own investment clubs. The book is structured around three core ideas: understanding your money story, identifying where to put your money and what to expect from each investment option, and knowing how to move forward. For Janine, the goal has always been about changing the world and making it a better place. She has come to realize that she wants to see how she can help women transform themselves, their financial security, and their impact.

Women currently control 50 percent of the money in this country, and that number is going to climb to 65 percent by 2030 and will probably continue to ascend over time. As Janine looks out twenty to thirty years, she predicts the majority of money in this country will be in the hands of women. The coming generations are quite different from the boomers and even the Gen Xers before them. Her challenge will be to help these generations make this trend a norm and not the case where men are threatened and women are boxed into roles and rules that no longer and maybe never made sense. These next generations of women will want to align their money with their values. While concerned about their financial returns, like Janine, they won't want to give up their values for those returns. Instead, they will want to put their money toward what matters the most so they can change the world for the better, one investment at a time.

From the Observation Deck

Janine's journey began with her early life experiences, in a family where she learned what it took to make a living, build a viable real estate business, and save for the future. Her story makes us ask important questions about how to raise our daughters. Robert Blum, professor at Johns Hopkins University and the director of the Global Early Adolescent study, found that regardless of what type of society they studied, children internalized myths at an early age. Girls who are taught to be submissive generally believe they are vulnerable and weak. Boys who are taught to take charge grow up to be strong and independent. Their findings set the stage for what has to be done to free girls from these norms and myths as they are growing up.

As we step back and look at the challenges for girls and the women they become, the research findings open problems we must address:

1. **First is the hegemonic myth.** Throughout the world, a set of forces from home, school, media, and peers reinforces the idea that girls are vulnerable, and boys are strong and independent. Parents who have bought into this myth focus on protecting, not educating, their daughters. Protection from harm appears to be essential and more comfortable to them than creating self-reliant women.

2. **Pubertal girls are the embodiment of sex and sexuality.** Societies around the world view boys as predators of girls. And those girls, in turn, are seen as potential victims. Messages such as "do not sit like that, do not wear that, or boys will ruin your future" support the gender division of power while promoting sex segregation to preserve a girl's purity. In some places, girls internalize these norms to even a greater extent than boys.

3. **As a result of these erroneous beliefs, in nearly every society, girls' mobility is far more restricted than boys.** Global research, qualitative and quantitative, captures the recurring theme that boys have the freedom to come and go as much as they would like. Whether to pursue education or friendships,

they are expected and empowered to demonstrate their ability to handle themselves outside of their homes. Girls, on the other hand, particularly as they enter puberty, find that their mobility is restricted. Silence and modesty, as well as limited freedoms, surround girls and young women to protect them from men and the world around them.

4. **Because of adult concerns about their sexual vulnerability, girls are repeatedly told to stay away from boys.** All types of sanctions are threatened and imposed if girls transcend these barriers, such as punishment, social isolation, sexual shaming, and innuendo. The boys and girls then have to make sense of why they once played together as children and were friends, and why now, with puberty, those friendships are no longer deemed acceptable and they must distance themselves from each other.

5. **Finally, boys and girls are aware of those who do not conform to these norms.** Such young people face significant pressures to conform to what society sees as gender-appropriate behaviors. And there are few places for girls who are tomboys or for boys who like to play with dolls.

Janine, and others like her, had a very different upbringing. Her mother taught her what is possible for a woman and how a woman can control her own destiny. Reflecting on my years growing up, my mother and grandmother taught me how to work in a family firm, how to earn and manage our money, and how to become a strong, professional woman. I didn't need to look far from my grandmother or my mother for successful role models. They had complicated daily lives in which they combined work with their roles in raising children and running the family. In time, I never thought women were only supposed to focus on the home. I certainly never thought I was going to marry a man and stay at home. Interestingly, my husband was raised by a professional mother and surrounded by accomplished aunts as well.

These role models can change our personal perceptions of our reality, along with our cultural values. With enough people, you can change a culture so that women begin to rethink the way they see themselves. They can change how they view money and manage it for themselves and their families. Girls can hear different stories about what they should become. Their brains can create mental maps that become their perceptual realities about what they are supposed to do and how they should do it. As they emerge as young women and grow into adulthood, they can learn how to manage their monies or those earned by a spouse. To help them become active managers of that money, we are going to have to change our stories to turn those women into our heroines, not vulnerable or in danger but strong and capable of leading productive, financially viable lives.

Janine offers us some valuable insights into how a woman's relationship with money develops and how we might be able to expand that relationship. Women can learn to make wise decisions about how to earn, save, and spend money. Janine's is a beautiful story about how life can allow you to create new ways of being.

If you don't learn the skills and confidence early in your development, it will be more difficult to change what you think you can do and how well you can do it later in life. If you are working to shift your perspective as an adult, these changes are going to need a supportive social structure, a community of others who support you as you try new ways of doing things.

The efforts Janine and others are making today around educating women about their financial investment strategies are only one step in overcoming a huge societal hurdle. Yet it is an essential one that can lay the foundation for the transformation of others. It is my hope that it will also reduce the anger and frustration that is underneath a great deal of male–female interactions and relationships around money today and that it will change the foundation of our society and the myths that control it.

Think about what you can do to change the way you are thinking about money. You are ready to write a new mythical story about how you are going to change. The goal is not to mimic men. It is to craft a new you—the financially wise woman. The new you can open up opportunities by believing that you can, indeed, earn a living and save wisely for your future and for that of others.

Women Do Not Make
Good College Presidents

"A man does what he can;
a woman does what a man cannot."

—*Isabel Allende*

I met Dr. Maria Gallo when I was invited to work with her university to help it find its Blue Ocean Strategy. Little did I know that I was going to be working with an amazing leader—someone who could see what was ahead and mobilize her faculty, board, and even her students to help the institution transform itself to get there.

My surprise was, in part, because of the work I had done before with institutions of higher education. I often found their presidents or leadership trying to incrementally improve upon the past. Their old styles focused on doing what they knew from before, but better. They did not seem to realize that the future was not going to look much like the past. It was time to rethink the university and recharge the institutions with new styles of leadership. Higher education was not going to thrive with the traditional, male-dominated, top-down controlling leader, or with faculty entrenched in their ways and always at odds with their administrations.

For higher education, the drivers of change are many. Only 20 percent of college students in 2019 are the traditional student, right out of high school. There are simply fewer students to draw from.

Of the other 80 percent of those turning to colleges and universities are those adults who need to sustain their value in the workforce through re-skilling. And educational institutions have to help businesses leverage the technology that is changing the worker and the workplace. For colleges and universities, a sustainable strategy is no longer "more of the same, at a higher price." It is a time for change—and perhaps that means a change in leadership.

In the context of these transformations, I had to wonder why there weren't more women leading higher education institutions. In 2020, only 38 percent of college presidents are women, despite the fact that women represent over half the students in colleges and universities and have since 1979. Women also have more than half the baccalaureate and doctoral degrees, yet the leadership teams of these 5,300 higher education institutions are typically male dominated, and their boards are rarely gender balanced.

The women who do become presidents of higher educational institutions tend to be leaders of two-year colleges or state schools, and only a small proportion of the more prestigious academic institutions have women in the C-suite office. In 2015, four of the Ivy League schools had women presidents—Elizabeth Garrett at Cornell University, Christina Paxson at Brown University, Drew Faust at Harvard University, and Amy Gutmann at the University of Pennsylvania. When Faust retired in 2018, that number dropped to three. And Faust was replaced by a man, Tufts University president Lawrence Bacow.

Perhaps we should be pleased at the number and percentage of women leading higher education institutions when we observe that in 2019, a grand total of thirty-three women headed Fortune 500 companies, making up 6.6 percent of the total. I had to wonder, were women doing better at universities than in large corporations?

The road for women to become presidents in higher education is not a simple straight line where they are identified early in their careers, mentored and grown, and shown how to reach this pinnacle. Instead, women seem to follow a maze of twists and turns to get to the top. Of course, this sounds like women should follow the road set by men. They should have a deep desire to lead. Women should be building their skills and their career to achieve positions of power and control. If they are going to compete with men for these positions, they should compete *like* men to attain them. But women are not men. Instead, women are following another path, often coming in to solve a crisis in an institution, and that is why Maria Gallo was such a perfect story to share.

All too often, women enter the presidency when the institution is in crisis. A greater percentage of women presidents than their male counterparts arrive in their jobs after serving as an interim president, in many cases after their male predecessor has left the institution in a major financial or political crisis. While that is not always the situation, what is clear is that new women presidents are finding themselves facing widespread challenges that require more than incremental improvements in the faculty, the programs offered, or a new Enterprise Resource Planning (ERP) system to integrate their software systems, streamline their operations, and improve the financial management. These institutions hiring women are often searching for a new leader, a heroine, because the old ways of operation are no longer working.

That is how Maria came to Delaware Valley University, in Doylestown, Pennsylvania. She is exactly that type of woman who did not aspire to be president of a university—yet here she is trying to turn DelVal (as it is called) around at a challenging time in higher education. Maria came to DelVal in 2016 to revitalize the institution. It needed new leadership to energize its faculty and staff. Maria was brought on to build an innovative university by implementing a new strategy and focus, with reenergized talent and hopefully the financial investment necessary to sustain its growth.

The approach Maria took reflects her own journey to become president of this university and her personal style for leading others. She offers an exceptional story. Her journey was not one driven by a desire to become a president of anything. Rather, her story is about how a woman wants to build and collaborate with others to create something bigger than any individual. Her skill at seeing what has to be done and mobilizing her talent to do it is exceptional—as is her story to share.

The Myth

The pressure on college presidents is quite intense today. There are many ideas about why women make up only a third of the presidents of universities and colleges. These ideas tend to fall into three stereotypes that people use to explain adversity and failure.

First is the myth that there aren't enough women in the pipeline to take on these presidential positions. The reality is the opposite. Women are highly educated today. Higher education is producing more women than men with degrees at all levels, as women represent over 60 percent of the students in these academic institutions. For the past thirty years, women have earned more than half the baccalaureate degrees. And over the last ten years, they have completed more than half of all doctoral degrees.

The second fallacy is that women don't know how to build their network, so they are not well-known to boards and leadership at academic institutions. In reality, women have moved up into chief academic officer and provost roles. They are highly invested in or hold positions of authority in associations for their disciplines or volunteering.

And the third myth is that women don't aspire to become presidents of these institutions and aren't well-trained in how presidents behave. Women suffer from these stereotypes. If they act strong and assertive, they are expected to either be bossy or bitches. If they collaborate, they are thought to be unable to make good decisions. If they populate their leadership team with more women than men, they are operating with a reverse bias. And men have no problem telling women how disappointed they are that the board selected them. As one woman president was told by her male subordinate, "If I had known they were really going to hire you, I would have joined the search committee so it would not have happened."

A major part of the problem is that men, be they faculty, staff, or board members, are uncomfortable working with strong women, and they are uncertain how their own careers will advance or be constrained by a different style of leadership. As men themselves often comment, they know how to build a team with a central, often autocratic leader. They know how to get them to stay on their toes, competing with one another for resources and for approvals. Women, however, lead differently. They work to encourage collaboration and cross-silo integration and to create a common focus on building the institution instead of separate areas.

The research and statistics on gendered organization offer a picture of what might come in the near future. Many practices in these male-dominated organizations have kept women out of the top ranks of leadership in both academics and administration. The "second shift" syndrome, where women are caught between their professional responsibilities and aspirations and the role in their families and their homes, has been a factor. Add to this the "invisible" job—where women have to play bigger roles in academic services—and the "hidden curriculum"—where they have to downplay their own successes to fit into the male culture, and women are fighting to find a pathway to positions where their skills and styles are needed and appropriate for today's institutions.

This means that when a woman does get recruited into the office, she has a lot of expectation "re-management" to go through. This often means re-skilling her team, creating new alignments, and building a culture that fosters different pathways and even different results. Their focus is beyond any individual, including themselves.

In the pages ahead, you will learn how Maria has been able to take her style, skills, and special appeal to convert her entire organization into one that is moving in new directions. As you read her story, take note of how women can achieve leadership roles via pathways that are quite different from those of men.

Meet Maria Gallo

Maria Gallo has one recurring refrain: "I never dreamed of becoming the president of a university." It was never in her story, her plans, or her aspirations. Rather, she was a curious and talented scientist who loved to discover new things.

Maria found us after one of her deans suggested they needed a new strategy. Her chief strategy officer, Roy Ortman, googled "Blue Ocean Strategy," and there we were. My company was hired soon after, and we began to work closely with Maria, Roy, faculty, leadership, board, staff, and even the students.

The idea of Blue Ocean strategic thinking is to stop competing in a bloody "red ocean" of vicious competition, in this case, a university serving over two thousand students offering a range of programs. Delaware Valley has a unique foundation for its educational programs and was founded as a "blue ocean." DelVal was founded in 1896 by Rabbi Joseph Krauskopf, an activist rabbi who was a tireless advocate for social justice. He purchased a one-hundred acre farm in Doylestown, arranged for the construction of a small classroom building, employed a faculty of two, and enrolled six students. With this modest start, the National Farm School (now Delaware Valley University) came into being.

Now the times were changing. DelVal had to find a new way to sustain its mission and grow its student body. It had a learn-by-doing approach and excellent student results. With a declining population of prospective students, DelVal was one of many universities competing for the same traditional student while also wondering who else was out there and needed them. DelVal had to leverage its position as one of the top twenty universities for animal sciences while offering a great deal more.

Maria's story sheds light on how a woman can grow herself into a leader. She picked up the problems she was dealt and led the way forward. That was what she was doing with DelVal and why we wanted to share her story. What is important about her life's journey was that she was always driven to achieve but not in the style of divide, conquer, and dominate. She always had a personal quest of self-improvement. And she never approached situations as if she knew everything or was the smartest person in the room. She was always eager to listen and learn, like a sponge soaking up the advice her mentors gave her, because they saw her potential to be a leader.

Growing up in the 1970s, Maria's early years were reflective of what made her tick. She grew up in a one-bedroom apartment. She pulled out a bed from the couch in the living room at night and had a small desk where she could do her homework. She loved school, and her parents encouraged her to focus, work hard, and do well. Her biggest interest, almost a passion then, was science. At an early age, she was drawn to science and particularly biology. Her father was a great inspiration. He had never gone to college, telling his daughter about his own reluctance to take high school honors classes because he would have to work too hard. But he never wanted Maria to follow him. As she recalled, he was always telling her stories about what she should not do.

Reading, particularly books about science, became her way of escaping. She'd go to the library on Saturdays and look at the shelves to read books. When she was eight years old, she began to frame in her mind where the best science came from—all the Ivy League schools and MIT. She made a list and put it on the corkboard above her desk. There she was as a young girl, promising herself that she was going to go to one of these universities.

When it came time to apply to colleges, she applied early to Cornell's College of Agriculture and Life Sciences. As a land-grant institution, this public college enabled her to receive in-state tuition. She was interested in the synergy of these two academic areas because of what was happening with the environment and with food production, and she wanted to learn how to produce food in a sustainable way. She became an agronomy major, admitting that she had "no idea what agronomy was as an incoming freshman, but from all the things I was interested in, they said this fit me the best."

This led her to focus on genetics. As she looked ahead to where the jobs were growing, she knew that biology was going to be about DNA and genes. She wanted to focus on plants and understand molecular biology and genetics. After graduating with her BS in agronomy from Cornell, Maria went to North Carolina State University for her master's and then her PhD, in crop science and genetics, respectively. As she was preparing to pursue her PhD, NC State was recruiting endowed professors called regents professors from across the country.

At NC State, she had supportive mentors, including one biochemistry professor, Dr. Frank Armstrong, who left a lasting impact. He told her about one of these regents professors and how he thought she would be a perfect fit for his new laboratory. Dr. Armstrong encouraged her to become a student of Dr. Bill Thompson, who had come from Stanford University to build a new research group. Maria joined his lab as a PhD graduate student, where she learned a great deal. She was able to develop her love of the sciences—everything about how to do cutting-edge science, how to teach it, and how to use science to answer the big questions.

After receiving her PhD, she joined Texas A&M for her postdoctoral work. She went out to Texas A&M's experimental station in

South Texas to work on sugarcane molecular biology. Maria was one of the first people in the world to genetically engineer sugarcane, a new field at the time.

While doing her postdoctoral work, Maria had another mentor who told her that if she wanted to move up the academic ladder beyond the faculty ranks, she had to take on more leadership roles, becoming involved in professional societies beyond presenting her science at meetings. Being modest yet bold, she volunteered. The scientific societies told her to show up and do whatever they needed her to do. Next thing she knew she was running graduate student competitions, becoming more familiar with the societies, and growing a network of influential people who came to know her and count on her. She got involved on scientific boards and reviewed articles for their publications, until she was nominated to become president of the Crop Science Society of America. Her first reaction was "Thank you, but no thank you."

However, another mentor, once again, encouraged her. "You have to do it," he said. "They are counting on you." From that moment on, she never looked back. Soon after, she became a fellow of both the American Society of Agronomy and the Crop Science Society of America.

Several things converged for Maria at this time in her life. She got her first faculty position at the University of Minnesota. It was a great time for her to be an assistant professor there while she became more active in the Crop Science Society of America and the American Society of Agronomy. Then the University of Florida was searching for a faculty member to join their agronomy department. Maria had the research experience in sugarcane, which as a tropical crop was not directly relevant to Minnesota agriculture but important to Florida. Maria applied and was hired for the University of Florida position, quickly moving up the ranks, making full professor.

During her time at Florida, Maria realized that to continue growing her skills, she should pursue a Fulbright scholarship and take a sabbatical. She sounded quite casual about this when we spoke, but it was a pivotal part of her career. She applied to be a Fulbright scholar in the Netherlands. After receiving her Fulbright, she headed to Utrecht University to teach and conduct research. This was one of the best experiences for her, as she grew her skills and confidence. As she remembers, "Here I was, all by myself in a foreign country and making friends and doing significant research. And that was great."

When Maria returned to Florida, she felt like an unofficial administrator, developing new ideas with people who were looking to make the university better. At that time, another of her mentors wanted her to become involved with a program to develop leaders for the land-grant universities. Called Lead21, it was a program designed to meet the needs for leadership development in the agricultural, environmental, and human sciences. Maria, in her modesty, told me how she was not clear what would be expected of her above and beyond her faculty responsibilities, but in her own way, she had decided she was going to take it on. Her dean for research willingly sponsored her for this eighteen-month national program. She was able to meet and work with people with all types of skills while taking leadership development workshops. During this time, she increased her professional skills and came to understand herself better as an influential leader. When her department needed an interim chair, she was the go-to choice, and most importantly, she was ready for it.

As Maria recalls, "I ran my research lab, and now I had this additional responsibility of being a chair. I didn't know whether I would like it or whether anybody would like me. I didn't even know if I'd be good at it. But I quickly realized that I loved being a part of that level of administration. I enjoyed working with the faculty."

It was also a time to develop a strategic plan for the department and for a national review of the program. Maria was part of the evaluation. When the department decided to hire a permanent chair, Maria threw her hat into the ring for the national search and was selected—her first taste of real senior administration at the University of Florida.

She'd been leading the program for several years when somebody nominated her for a dean's position at the University of Hawaii. She decided to apply for the position on the last day for submitting applications. When Hawaii called her, she was surprised and flattered. It was a hard decision. She had built a home in Florida, where she had spent much of her career. Florida was exactly what she wanted. How could she move? But the opportunity had come, and she realized she could not pass it up. So she interviewed, and with her talent and experience, she was hired.

After four years in Hawaii, she felt it was time to get back to the Northeast, closer to her family. Delaware Valley came calling. Maria saw DelVal as an opportunity to take a small but excellent university and provide it with a renewed energy, direction, and excitement. Her approach was telling. The first thing she did was listen and try to understand where everybody was—from students, faculty, administration, and the community. She wanted to know what was going well and where the problems were. She worked to prioritize and determine what to focus on first, as well as what would move the entire institution forward, fast.

What she saw was an encouraging desire to change. Everyone at DelVal wanted to be led somewhere new, with someone who had a bold enough vision to take them there. They wanted to feel valued and believe that the university had a purpose beyond just another place. What she didn't want to do was have too many initiatives operating all at once without a clear strategy. She knew that the world was changing quickly. As a small college with unique niches, they had to capitalize on their uniqueness. And that was where the Blue Ocean Strategy came in.

When I watched Maria lead her team through the process, I

saw how inclusive she was. She was completely involved in the process. She encouraged ideas, built confidence in the ability of others to implement those new ideas, and enabled her entire organization, from the board to the administration to faculty and others, to visualize what was coming so they could make it happen.

Maria had developed a highly effective leadership style. She told me she "liked a facilitative approach," stating that was her tendency. She then added, "Sometimes, you have to be decisive and top-down depending on if it's something that needs a really quick decision where you can't wait for consensus and getting everybody together."

Many times, we watched as she pulled everybody back to ask them what was best for the student. Her focus became that of the entire university and what was going to give the best quality education. What Maria loves about DelVal are the staff and the faculty. She adds, "They're very student-centric. That's why they're here. It's not about their personal programs. They really love teaching."

Maria has also been strategic about working with her board. She has collaborated with them to rebuild that board. She works with them closely on a constant basis, keeping them informed of her thoughts about where they are going and how they are achieving their objectives. During my work with them, the board became closely involved, helping to discover unmet needs and potential new markets for DelVal.

Maria often hears people wondering how she can be so devoted, working long hours, and always on top of what is happening at the university. She says she loves what she does. She doesn't even think she is working long hours. In some ways, all of her curiosity as a researcher comes through. She listens, watches, tests, and watches some more. Looking for what works and how to nourish it, she doesn't overthink what others are trying to achieve. A university is a complex ecosystem that needs energy and focus, hope, and many small wins to move forward. She brings a testing mindset to others and enables them to keep trying, just a bit harder.

One area I found most exciting was how she built upon the legacy of an institution that teaches learning by doing. DelVal had an excellent Experience 360 program when my team arrived there. It enabled students to have active learning or internships. One of the realizations of our work was that the value of that active learning ought to permeate the entire university and become part of its core focus. Maria believed that experiential learning could be a big differentiator, and together, with faculty and her team, they began to rethink their entire approach to learning. She brought things full circle for the university, realizing that everything should be built on the learning-by-doing approach that Dr. Krauskopf envisioned back in 1896. Perhaps that was the key to DelVal's success.

DelVal also had exceptional results placing students in jobs and graduate or professional schools after they graduated. More than 92 percent of their students had positions or were furthering their education after graduation. As I worked together with Maria, I saw that job placement was never an afterthought; it was *the* thought. The entire purpose of the university was to enable students to find excellent employment, hopefully in jobs they desired, and that was what DelVal achieved, helping graduates find positions with biotech and pharmaceutical companies, as well as teaching and criminal justice jobs. Having worked with other institutions, I knew that this focus was extraordinary and its success remarkable.

The power of a leader is in gaining the confidence of their followers. They will move in new directions if they believe their leader can visualize where they should be going and help them formulate an actionable plan to get there. That was exactly how Maria Gallo inspired her faculty and staff. And she knew how to motivate them, educate them, and demonstrate to them the challenges that lay ahead and how they could overcome them. She is a leader that sells a powerful vision and helps others play a role in achieving that vision.

From the Observation Deck

Having been a tenured professor, and having many university clients, we were not surprised by the challenges facing Maria Gallo when she took over DelVal. Universities, as I have heard so often, think of themselves as above and beyond other businesses. Faculty often would say they aren't a business, that they are there to educate students. They aren't exactly a monastery, but at times they sound priestly. Their job takes them, in their minds, beyond the needs of the everyday business of education. Faculty have to tend to the needs of their students.

That might be true for the faculty, but it is hardly the case for those running the university. While she had to respect and protect the faculty, Maria had to navigate a business turnaround during tough times. She, like other presidents of challenged businesses, had to rethink who were going to be her customers—those students of tomorrow—and how to best attract and retain them. One thing was clear: demography is destiny, and the number of traditional students was not growing. Consequently, DelVal was going to have to become a highly innovative organization.

Further, Maria had to navigate with thin margins while rethinking her programs and enhancing her marketing, branding, and communications. The university had to tell a new story over and over again, internally and externally. She had to transform the relationship of the university with the surrounding community while engaging the faculty and students and merging it all into something that could thrive in fast-changing times.

Maria also had an excellent board that was essential in helping to raise significant dollars for the new programs and converting untapped resources into valuable revenues. The board members also had to see a new future for the institution.

She had a big opportunity or a significant problem. Like so many leaders, she was on the brink of either soaring or falling. Maria had the energy, grace, and people skills to mobilize her troops and free their enthusiasm to sustain their growth. That was, of course, before COVID-19 created a new world for higher education. The future is always uncertain, and it is particularly unclear for DelVal and all the midsize universities trying to serve their audiences in innovative ways during and after a pandemic shutdown.

Is Maria a unique individual? Of course. Can she be a role model for other women? Absolutely. As a leader, her biggest achievement, from my perspective, is how her team, faculty, board, and students became motivated, mobilized, and inspired. It was quite inspiring even to us, the consultants.

When I see what Maria has achieved, I wonder about the research that suggests that women don't aspire to be presidents of colleges. It may be true, and unfortunate, that many women aren't convinced they are presidential material. They lack champions who help open doors and build the necessary networks. And talented women cannot overcome the recurring biases that influence the attitudes of boards and faculties who are discounting them as they search for new leadership.

Somehow, Maria did what women weren't supposed to do and did it without intentionality. She focused on what mattered to her. She had the talent and self-motivation, and her mentors provided options and opportunities. She proved that women do not have to mimic what men do to become inspiring leaders. Instead, they can pursue their own passions while capturing the trust of others, helping them see what is possible.

What I love about Maria's story, as she shared it, was her being malleable while her mentors advised, pushed, and encouraged her into new territory. She never spoke about being overwhelmed or over her head. Each new position was something she was interested in exploring. She was a great discoverer and yet also able to motivate others to follow her lead.

Equally interesting was how she was never in any pipeline during her journey—at least in her own mind. Rather, she was fully committed to the moment. She sustained her passion for science and research, capitalizing on her understanding of how she was part of a larger community that needed to collaborate better to achieve its goals.

When I look at statistics and realize that only one-third of our universities and colleges have women leaders, you have to wonder why. It is time to better support women so they recognize themselves as visionaries, capable of mobilizing others to follow them, together, to new places. Women may lead through more collaborative approaches, engaging people in a process of transformation. They may not always be that top-down leader. Women like Maria lead differently, but effectively, by building teams that trust each other to work toward common goals. With the pressure on institutions of higher education today, this type of leader and the imperative to build them will lead to real solutions.

It's up to us to figure out how to navigate this new path, with all its turns and twists. And with the right guidance, it can be a path that we can navigate successfully. While there may be challenges and stereotypes to overcome along the way, it is up to us to take the first step into this new territory, for this is how we grow.

Are you a woman who sees herself achieving more than what you have or are doing right now? Are people telling you that you can achieve something more? If so, are you grabbing ahold of the rope to see where it takes you? Or are you digging a hole to avoid the risk? Your future is up to you. And it is my hope that you will follow in Maria's footsteps and take the risk.

Women Can't Be Geoscientists

"As in geology, so in social institutions,
we may discover the causes of all past changes in the
present invariable order of society."

—*Henry David Thoreau*

When Evelyn Medvin was in high school, she took a class in earth sciences because she wanted to avoid the chemistry teacher with an unsavory reputation. What she discovered in this class became her lifelong calling and field of study. After college, Evelyn became a geoscientist. Then and even today, geoscience is a profession that remains less than friendly toward women. But it is changing. Evelyn has been working hard to help women improve the field and the acceptance of women professionals in it. The geosciences need them. Women need the respect and equality they deserve as talented professionals in a field that is projected to grow 16 percent by 2025.

Evelyn never seemed to pay much attention to hurdles she might have to leap over or the closed doors and glass ceilings she might face in the ranks of leadership in an industry that was dominated by men. She seemed to have a special talent: an almost intuitive feel for geology, since she could see geology in seismic waveforms that reflect the subsurface of the earth. She also ignored the limitations of being a woman in a field of men. Instead, Evelyn pushed forward into an industry that was learning how to include women in their technical workforce. Women were often thought to be too fragile to head into the field or stay in rough campsites, exploring for oil and gas. Evelyn was among those women who were quite happy trucking out into the field, whether on seismic crews in Louisiana or Ecuador. She crafted an exceptional career and shared her success with other women to help them succeed as geoscientists in a world still uncertain of their capabilities.

Evelyn was quick to share the way in which men were key mentors to her at a time when there were few women in the industry. Her male advisors, trainers, and colleagues each seemed to capture the spirit of her calling. They encouraged her, found ways to train and support her, and helped her develop the confidence needed to lead others in this field. They weren't the bad guys. The problem, in part, was that too few women had been exposed to the field, and fewer still chose to pursue careers in it. As she noted, "Someone better want to change something, or not much is going to happen."

I met Evelyn through a wonderful client of mine, Paul Grossbard, who happens to be Evelyn's brother. It was with great pride and admiration that he introduced us, after mentioning what a wonderful story she had to share. Let's take a look at the history of this field and see how Evelyn was able to smash away some of the "we don't do that" mythology and push forward with passion and professional success.

The Myth

The path forward is never simple or straightforward. In the nineteenth century, women were thought to be too weak and unable to work in the earth sciences. Some of the traditional folklore was telling. While girls and women were indulged occasionally in fieldwork, they were thought to be far too weak to do serious work. Some women became fossil collectors and dealers. One of significant note was Mary Anning (1799–1847), who built a successful career as a fossil collector, dealer, and paleontologist. She became known around the world for her important finds of Jurassic marine fossil beds. Her findings contributed to significant changes in how science thought about prehistoric life. However, it took until 2010 for the Royal Society to include Anning in a list of the ten British women who have most influenced the history of science.

In the twentieth century, the number of female geoscience college enrollments began to climb, particularly after the 1960s as women found earth sciences, geology, oceanography, and related sciences attractive areas for study and careers. The numbers of women in the geosciences climbed steadily from the 1970s through the early 2000s. Then the growth paused and flattened out for a number of reasons.

First, while the ability of women to get jobs in the geosciences and move up into higher-level positions was improving, difficulties remained. Women were still seen as not being as competent as men. Further, they also were seen as outsiders and not a good fit for the boys' club. And the old stereotypes of men needing to be in charge so women could have babies still held strong.

Today, entering the field remains challenging for women. They feel their salaries are too low, opportunity for advancement is slight, and senior positions are controlled by men. The ongoing biases and discrimination by those men are undermining women's belief in their value in these fields. Additionally, these women have few women mentors or role models. In short, women find the field lonely.

How, then, did Evelyn Medvin become a successful, award-winning, and highly respected geoscientist? In part, she just did it. Never in her story does she ponder the challenges she faced. She credits the mentoring and support she received, often from men. While there were few women in the field in the 1980s, Evelyn was sought after as a student, trainee, and colleague by men who saw her talent and encouraged her growth in the industry. Then she saw the need to help other women create networks, mentors, and business cultures where they could thrive in an otherwise unwelcoming industry that she is working to change.

Let's look at her story and think about the myths and her personal journey to break through them to create a life with purpose in a field she felt was her calling.

Meet Evelyn Medvin

Evelyn grew up in Tulsa, Oklahoma, where she discovered her accidental career. In her senior year in high school, 1976, an oil company, Cities Service Oil Company, known to the public as Citgo, wanted to give back to its community. They sponsored an Explorer Post program in geology that included Edison High School, which Evelyn attended. They did all types of activities, including a two-week trip to Colorado and New Mexico, visiting meteor craters, ice caves, dormant volcanoes, and the Grand Canyon. The company sent a geologist with them, and they had a grand old time exploring the earth.

People don't realize Oklahoma has four different mountain ranges. They're old, eroded, and made for great geological places to visit. Evelyn would get up at 6:00 in the morning on a Saturday or a Sunday, put on her gear and hiking boots, and pack a lunch. When it came time to go to college and she didn't know what to study, her parents looked at her and said, "Are you kidding? What do you mean you don't know what to study? What other high school kids get up at 6:00 in the morning to look at rocks?"

On one of their trips, Evelyn asked if Cities Service ever hired students in college for summer internships. The group advisor went back and checked. While they did, they only hired employee children as a perk. Evelyn suggested he talk to their administration about the money they had invested in the explorer club and their summer excursion. Making the return-on-investment case, she was able to convince them to hire her and another student, and they were the first two employees who did not have parents working at Cities Service. Later that year, Evelyn changed her major in college from education to geology. She worked for Cities Service every summer while in college and is still in touch with some of the people who were her mentors that summer. Over the years, some even became clients.

Evelyn studied at the University of Oklahoma and became what she loved: a geoscientist. Two advisors—one from academia and the other from industry—guided Evelyn through her senior thesis. The thesis involved the study of coral reefs in the Caribbean, where she spent many hours in laboratories making measurements.

Her academic advisor encouraged her to get involved in the campus chapter of the American Association of Petroleum Geologists (AAPG). As the chapter's vice president, Evelyn began to develop her style and leadership skills.

Her other, more industry-focused advisor had her submit an abstract for AAPG's first student paper contest. He threatened to withhold her grade if she didn't submit one. To her surprise the paper was accepted, and she received second place in the competition, along with an A from her professor.

She laughs as she remembers almost flunking physics, even with a tutor. She remembers her grades coming to her at the company. "They were like, 'Oh, what's this D?'" Somehow, she was able to explain it away and managed to get hired into their training program in Tulsa. The bulk of the training was in geophysics, which focused on studying seismology, natural earthquakes, and seismic data. She worked using seismic data to map the subsurface of the earth, telling companies where to drill or not to drill to find hydrocarbons.

After college, she went to work for Cities Service as a geophysicist in the South and Central America Region. Evelyn had a real skill blending her geological knowledge with her understanding of the earth. She was practically trained, rather than theoretically trained, and could bring it all together, and it worked. As Evelyn shared, "I could do it, because that's the way my brain works. I had six months of training in Tulsa. Then I put down international as my first assignment choice, which all my mentors at the company said I probably wouldn't get because that was typically reserved as a perk for people who had five years' experience. But I got it and was assigned to the Latin America group, so I moved to Houston in 1981."

When Cities Service Oil and Gas was acquired by Occidental Petroleum in 1983, Evelyn realized that Occidental typically only hired people with a master's degree and five years of experience. Evelyn had neither and was concerned about her career future. Yet with her three years' work experience Occidental kept her on, and she moved out to Bakersfield, California. She was twenty-four at the time, on her way, but never sure where she was heading.

Evelyn's career was fast-tracking. She worked with Occidental's Latin America Exploration team from 1983 through 1991. In 1991, she became a senior geophysicist for the Far East Division with Occidental International Exploration and Production Company (OIEPC), working offshore in Malaysia. From August 1991 to May 1995, as a senior geophysicist, she worked on projects across the US.

While in Bakersfield, Evelyn met her husband, Roger, at her synagogue and never looked back. They had two children. Her husband built his advertising/public relations business, and she continued to develop her career.

Evelyn had some important and illustrative stories to share about the experiences that transformed her as she crafted her skills and developed her career. During her early years, she was part of several international projects that were searching and developing hydrocarbon reserves. She had an integral role in the Cano Limon Discovery in Colombia. This discovery enabled Colombia to move from a hydrocarbon importing country to an exporting country. During her work there, she could not gain access to go out in the field as part of the seismic field crew because of kidnappings of oil field workers. Redeployed to jungles in Ecuador, she went out into those fields to develop her experience searching for oil. Her story, however, highlights the challenges women faced in the field.

Travel in Ecuador was by helicopter, the only way to get around. Accommodations in the four-hundred-person camp were mainly huts arranged in a protected area of the jungle. But Evelyn loved the adventure. She told one of the helicopter pilots that she wished there was a chair to sit on, not just the benches that were in the jungle camp. Before long, a one-of-a-kind high-back chair arrived, painted white just for Evelyn. As she recalled, no one else dared to sit on that chair.

Evelyn came away from this experience excited, better skilled, and technically poised for the next jobs to be done. She continued to explore for oil and gas in various Latin American countries and in the US. Following her passion for new technologies, she began to work with others to employ computer-aided interpretation technologies to improve evaluations of the subsurface, make better-informed decisions, and locate more accurate drilling site locations.

During this time, she had to remain true to herself and honest to her industry. Evelyn's job was to put the facts together, stay above the line, and find oil. One story that captured her dilemma quite nicely was the pressure to identify sites for oil drilling where she did not think there was anything in the ground. She would study the geology and seismic maps, lay out the places to drill for oil, assess the risk factors, and then convince others not to make mistakes.

Sometimes, she would have to show them that if they drilled a well in a particular location, they would have a dry hole. They would argue with her, saying, "Why do you say that?" when they had already committed to drilling a well on a particular lot. She had to persuade them to get another drilling location or they would come up dry. They would push her, and she would say, with some humor and a lot of gumption: "OK. Give me a rubber band." The men, puzzled, would ask, "What do you mean?" to which she would reply, "Give me a rubber band."

After receiving the rubber band, she would shoot it at the map and say, "Drill there!" They would look at her, once again puzzled. "What are you doing?" And she would reply, "It doesn't matter where you drill. It is going to be dry. If you are doing this for political reasons, go ahead. Any spot is fine, because they are all going to be dry holes."

She and Roger decided to move back to Houston in 1995. She was ready to come back to what felt like a home for herself and her family. Somehow, she would figure out a way to sustain her career. At the time, Occidental Petroleum was reducing its staff. There were no jobs for her in the traditional oil and gas operator companies. So she decided to look into the service company business and chose to work for Schlumberger/GeoQuest, where she became the expert in seismic interpretation workstations.

When Evelyn joined Schlumberger/GeoQuest in the marketing department in Houston, specializing in 3D visualization interpretations, she also represented the company with their global customers onsite and through technical conferences, presentations, and publications. She quickly took to the new technology, teaching customers how to use it. What she learned was that she could assist sales people by explaining the systems and how they would benefit customers. Since she was the expert, she knew what the technology could do and quickly realized she was good at teaching others, both inside the company and outside clients.

In July 1997 she joined Coherence Technology Company as vice president of interpretation services. She was responsible for the interpretations of their proprietary Coherence Cube™ worldwide. She had reached the stage where she had expertise with 3D seismic interpretations in the three-dimensional workspace to integrate technology into the exploration and production workflow, optimizing drilling locations and impact. She had developed this mix of technical expertise and client communication skills so the technology could be deployed and understood and the results properly acted upon in the field.

She worked with Coherence for almost three years, which helped her hone her skills in business development. Evelyn loved working with clients, helping them sell their ideas and solutions in ways that worked. It captured her imagination and allowed her to grow in her business development role. Then Core Laboratories bought the company in 1999. Evelyn became their vice president for business development and the technical coordinator for the Americas from 2000 to 2002. In 2002 she became vice president of corporate business development, a position she still holds today. Now she is leading intracompany teams on the technology and business needs of key customers while also bringing in or developing client relationships and new revenue, increasing current client accounts. Her perspective across the organization and her focus on the needs of clients enabled her to build teams that could effectively serve their clients with purposeful solutions for reservoir optimization.

She established herself as someone who could effectively present, collaborate, and engage, as well as offer the technical expertise and experience that clients required and internal teams expected. What is important is that she grew in great part because of the men who saw her skills, trusted her judgment, and learned with her in a fast-changing field. There were few women to mentor other women. All along the way, men in the field encouraged her, showed her the ropes, and let her learn new technology and new ways of sharing it, building her skills and confidence. Whether the teachers early in her development, the men in the field who built her that white chair, or the colleagues in Bakersfield or Houston, they knew that she had what it took and followed her, and she had the style to lead them collaboratively and confidently. They encouraged this woman leader and joined with her to move the industry forward.

As her positions changed, Evelyn became a voice for her companies and for the industry—and for women's roles in geosciences. Core Laboratories was supportive of Evelyn creating an offsite for female customers to network and build a group of like-minded females they could rely on and reach out to as mentors and sounding boards.

Evelyn made numerous presentations, having discovered that she is an inspirational public speaker. She has published several articles on oil and gas technology applications and is an active member and leader in several professional industry organizations. She also enjoys mentoring women and young people interested in oil and gas careers and works with high school students to encourage them to go into STEM programs.

In 2017, she was selected as one of the recipients of the BioHouston Women in Science Award. The support of her customers made her the first woman from an oil and gas service company to earn this award—and that is what made it most meaningful. And in 2019, the American Association of Petroleum Geologists presented her with the Distinguished Service Award for her long-term service to AAPG and her support of women and men in the industry through this global organization.

Evelyn is a member of the Independent Producers Association of America/Petroleum Equipment Supplier Association Education board, which is dedicated to bringing knowledge of STEM studies to high school students. Through this effort, she connects with students to share her journey and enthusiasm for the industry and to remind them that anything is possible.

Evelyn's roles as wife, mother, and grandmother are her most cherished, and she considers her son and daughter among her greatest successes. Her daughter moved to a foreign country at age twenty and earned a master's in archaeology while becoming a licensed tour guide, wife, and mother. Her son went in a different direction—and he has a Super Bowl ring to prove it. He handles media relations for the Denver Broncos. What a thrill it was to see her son standing on the sidelines at one of the world's major sporting events with an audience of millions. When people ask her what the industry is going to look like in the future, she tells them that she honestly doesn't know. What she does know is that the future is ours to create.

From the Observation Deck

Evelyn was a highly trained, field-experienced geoscientist who rose throughout her life by helping her firms and others expand their knowledge and build their skills. She was a subject-matter expert (SME). Today, the SME has become a driver of growth for many organizations. Over the past decade, in the business-to-business, or B2B, world in particular, businesses find that their clients would much rather deal with and buy from an SME than a typical salesperson. Expertise has risen to the top of what is needed for a business to succeed.

This transition reflects how knowledge workers are of critical importance for business success. As you look at your organization, do you have people who, like Evelyn, can "see" it—whether it is a problem to be solved or the way you can resolve it? Businesses recognize that the talent required goes well beyond static basics. To sustain and develop their global workforces, companies are opening digital universities and encouraging staff to expand their knowledge base and share their learnings. And they are watching as a business's growth comes from the expertise that is spread over an organization, not held within silos.

As Evelyn helped others turn their technology into understandable and useful solutions for clients, she grew, enjoying new roles and continuously expanding her value. She never stopped reinventing herself. And it kept working for her and for her organizations.

As I read through the abundant literature on women in the geosciences and thought about Evelyn's journey, I couldn't help but wonder what women need to do to push beyond the walls, ceilings, and other roadblocks that men set up for them—or that women create for themselves. Evelyn succeeded, and others will as well, in some part due to their own efforts. She clearly had an ability to overcome industry limitations. Today, there is growing support from organizations committed to helping women like Evelyn move forward. It is a broad, team approach to change the way women and men see themselves in this field. These women need to ignore what others say they can or cannot do—and simply push forward.

Today, only 6 percent of the CEOs of energy companies are women, and fewer than 25 percent are in the C-suite roles that might be a pipeline to get them into those CEO jobs, except for the chief human resource officers. Across a thousand major corporations, more than 50 percent of the chief human resource officers are women, and it is the only area where there is parity.

To be able to change the myth and the culture that supported it, we must turn to several crucial areas:

- Changing the system and the culture that embraces the values, beliefs, and actions of today

- Building social networks (of men and women) where women can find like-minded individuals who understand them and help them pursue careers

- Providing recognition—not just monetary rewards but also the public recognition that people need to celebrate their accomplishments with others

When I work with organizations that need to change, I speak about the process that people go through to resist the changes and then slowly move through the transformation. First, people need to see others changing. As mimics, we are uncomfortable outliers and rarely trust that something new is going to be better than what we have now—that is, until we see others changing and learn it is safe to try.

Second, people need to know why they need to change. Their brains need something to tie into their open personal perceptions of reality and must understand the "why" for the changes. They are much happier resisting and letting their brains hijack the new than embracing it and not knowing how to do it. Fear of failure is powerful, so we need to train and show people how to do new things. When you are learning something new, you need a lot of practice and support, which is why mentors are so vital to helping you move forward. That is why the work that Evelyn and others are doing with high school students is so important.

And last, we need to restructure the social organization, the rewards and recognition, and the ways we celebrate success in this industry. For the geosciences, this is a slow-moving process. Because of this, we need more wind behind the geoscience sails and more people like Evelyn to show others the way.

For more women to move up the ranks in these industries, leaders are going to have to change major elements of their cultures and the myths supporting them. When we reflect on Evelyn's career, her success came from many directions. In our conversations, Evelyn reflected repeatedly on how the men she worked with accepted her and encouraged her development. She had a remarkable ability to "see geology," and they admired and respected her skills. Together they shared her success.

But equally important is her ability to help other women network in her industry. As Evelyn began to see her own strengths and skills, she became a builder of people, of companies, and of society. She continues to do it with passion and purpose. She made her way through a thicket of obstacles and achieved her personal and professional success despite them. Smashing a myth and changing a culture is not an easy row to hoe, but once opened, other women can come rushing through.

Are you ready?

Women Aren't Fit
for Careers in Aerospace

"I was annoyed from the start by the attitude of doubt by
the spectators that I would never really make the flight. This
attitude made me more determined than ever to succeed."

—*Harriet Quimby, prior to her flight across
the English Channel, 1912*

How does a woman ever get into aerospace, much less create her
own successful business in an industry that has been harsh to women?
Celeste Ford is that woman. She has been a highly successful female
engineer in aerospace from the early days of the industry, and she
turned her skills and perspective into an entrepreneurial business.
Her company, Stellar Solutions, is a twenty-five-year-old, woman-led
consulting firm in the aerospace sector that solves complex problems—and does it well.

Perhaps due to a bit of luck, timing, and risk, a career as an aerospace engineer became the perfect fit for Celeste. Celeste wasn't
entirely sure how she got into this industry, where women aren't
typically found. More often, women occupy support roles instead
of technical ones. And they frequently are frustrated by the implied
meritocracy, which is driven by stereotypes and biases about what
women can and should be doing in general and in the industry.

I met Celeste at a Vistage International workshop where I was teaching Blue Ocean Strategy. She and one of her vice presidents bought into the strategy immediately, and we held a retreat with her management team to talk about how they could use the process to create a new market for Stellar. They understood Blue Ocean Strategy because they were already seeing their worlds in terms of blue oceans, or new market spaces and opportunities.

In fact, Celeste's entire work life has centered on creating new markets for herself, for those companies where she worked, and for her own company—all around the aerospace sector. Her story excited me because of how she saw the world. Her lens was open and expanding. The limitations that might hold others back inspired her to take a running start and leap over them. As I listened to Celeste sharing her story, I knew that while aware of her achievements, she is a woman more interested in celebrating the success of her clients and her employees. She is a wonderful individual who is bursting through those walls and building a new reality, or myth, for others to follow. Her story needed to be told for other women to see how they could shatter those myths, biases, and stereotypes and find their way in the aerospace world—one that ultimately needs their talent and ingenuity.

The Myth

The myth is that women are not right for aerospace or aeronautics. The aerospace sector (military aircraft, missiles, space, commercial airliners, and general aviation) is not exactly a female-friendly world. By 2012, only about 10 percent of aerospace engineers and computer network architects were women. Over the last twenty years, the percentage of women in aerospace has held steady. Only 16 percent of the aircraft, spacecraft, and manufacturing subgroup within aerospace are women. Of those, most are in support roles, administration, program management, and finance, not engineering or leadership. The airline industry is not much better. In December 2018, Air France, for example, *just* appointed the first woman CEO in the industry, Anne Rigail, with the task to bring the unions together and avoid future strikes. In a 2018 meeting of the International Air Transport Association board of governors, which represents 290 airlines and 82 percent of global air traffic, there was one woman among twenty-six airline bosses: Christine Ourmières-Widener, CEO of small regional UK carrier Flybe Group Plc. Additionally, only 4.4 percent of pilots are women.

Ironically, women were an important force during the early years of these industries. And perhaps they can become that force again. The problem is more than just the culture and biases of the industry. The larger problem is that women are not entering the field. The prevailing argument is that women like to work with people, while men gravitate toward working with things. The aerospace industries have a male-dominated culture. Beyond the idea of a meritocracy, there is the gender bias and stereotyping that work against women entering this industry.

This is a huge challenge. Women are going to have to push into and over the hurdles that the male-dominated industry has created, to topple the belief system that justifies why these women are neither capable nor welcome. As Susan Chodakewitz wrote in 2012, the reason more women aren't attracted to the industry is that they are uncertain or frightened about moving into a field where there aren't role models, a history of gender bias exists, and the lack of community might make them feel unwelcome as part of an industry where their talent belongs.

There is some hope in the trends and needs identified by analyses of the workforce. The number of women in aerospace and defense careers is on the rise. In 2014, after much effort to improve the diversity of the aerospace and defense workforce, 10.5 percent of the engineering executives and 17.9 percent of the software and development employees were women. The larger issue goes deeper, into engaging women in

STEM training and demonstrating to them that careers in aerospace offer opportunities and a culture that respects and rewards them. Programs such as those at the University of Michigan are counting on women faculty to build a community of women who are training for and interested in belonging to the aerospace industry.

Maybe there is something happening outside of the mainstream industry itself. Maybe there are talented women who can create a new market space for other women. Can Celeste Ford offer a model for others to emulate in an industry that needs more women—and *fast*—as the boomers retire and the demand intensifies for talent industry-wide?

Meet Celeste Ford

Celeste has a great story to share. Back in her youth in Colorado, she grew up in a home where her father was an FBI agent, and she moved around a lot. The high school she was attending had a strong program in math and science. Everyone would say to her, "Well, if you're good in math and science, you should be an engineer." However, she had no idea what an engineer was. And during the 1970s, there was no internet to google unfamiliar concepts.

As she tells it, this is the unglamorous story of aerospace as her choice, because everyone expected her to say something like, "I looked up at the stars and the moon and was inspired to become an astronaut." As it turns out, she was good at math and science because she went to a good school. With each additional engineer she spoke with, the less she understood what they did, because she had no frame of reference. She didn't have any role models at home, because no one in her family was an engineer. Then, when she opened the college catalog under engineering, the first line was "aerospace."

When I asked her about this choice, she said, "Not that it was that silly or simple. I didn't say, 'Oh, I'll pick the first one,' but it rang true to me. I had this 'aha!' moment, and something struck a chord with me. I can still feel it. I thought, 'If I'm going to go to college, I'm going to learn something totally different. I've been there, done that with English and history. It's not going to change, it's just relearning. But I don't know anything about aerospace engineering. That would be a fun new thing to learn.'"

Celeste picked aerospace engineering as a major and applied to several colleges, eventually choosing the University of Notre Dame. At the time, Notre Dame had one of the leading undergraduate programs in this field. This was the 1970s, when everyone was being laid off in aerospace, so people were questioning that as a career choice. But by her senior year, she had been wined and dined from coast to coast due to the lack of aerospace engineers graduating in America. It is always interesting to see how these types of gaps can be an opportunity for women to fill, as long as they are willing to take a risk and jump in.

For Celeste, the timing was perfect, as was the school. Notre Dame had a wonderful program where Celeste received a lot of personal attention, unlike at the larger schools. Celeste adds, "You had the actual teacher teaching you, not a grad student. You still had grad students there—but they were more support than anything else—and a lot of fun, hands-on labs, wind tunnels, and building stuff. It was great. Then, of course, Notre Dame is just great for growing the whole person, so I felt like that was a wonderful experience."

Celeste accepted her first job in California working for COM-SAT, the Communication Satellite Corporation. Coincidentally, she had always wanted to go to Stanford. And there she was in Palo Alto, so she said, as if merely checking off an extra item on her to-do list, "I should just get my master's while I'm at it."

Celeste was accepted into Stanford, and while working full time, she earned her master of science degree in aerospace engineering. At COMSAT, she was in charge of the guidance and control subsystem, which was built in Germany. She traveled to Germany for testing and development and then returned to Palo Alto to work on the subsystem that was integrated into larger satellites. Then she would travel with her equipment to Florida for a launch and to Washington, DC, to the control center. While a first job, it exposed her to the players in the budding commercial and international space industry. Because this was a time when the industry was emerging, it needed innovators and creative individuals who could figure out a problem and solve it, regardless of its complexity.

The project she was working on was called Intelsat, managed by an international consortium. Every country was represented with equipment, so it was a great opportunity to learn, one-on-one, about global business and aerospace. Looking back, it was quite a first job for Celeste—maybe not for everybody, but perfect for her. While a commercial program, it had a fast timeline, with construction and launch in three years. While others might have been overwhelmed by the scope, the travel, and the sophistication of the project, it all fit perfectly into Celeste's personality and style.

From her perspective, the position at COMSAT was a starting point, not an end or a place to stop growing. At the time, she remembers always thinking, "What's next?" It just so happened that one of her coworkers was married to someone who worked for the Aerospace Corporation. This was a company she had interviewed with previously, but she had been turned down because she didn't have a master's degree at the time. Now she had one. Celeste shared that she never wanted some obstacle to keep her from getting her dream job, and she didn't.

The Aerospace Corporation was just down the street from COMSAT, and they worked with the Department of Defense on satellites. She remembers thinking, "They must be doing some really high-tech, cool stuff that we commercial international people don't do, so that would be a natural next step."

After she built and launched several Intelsat satellites for COM-SAT, she applied and went to work for Aerospace Corporation. There she was assigned to NASA's Space Shuttle program, because the missions being worked were civil space programs and not classified at the time (she did not have a security clearance). The Department of Defense (DOD) was just getting on board with the space shuttle, and no one at DOD was interested in working on it, as none of the satellites that required security clearances had been assigned to shuttle missions, but all that would change.

At the time, Celeste was the new kid. Her boss departed the company within a couple of weeks, leaving her as the dedicated person for the program at Aerospace. Aerospace was responsible for writing the documents for and interfacing with all the people from DOD who were going to work on the classified DOD shuttle missions, including the astronauts. Once again, this was a great job, especially for a young woman. Celeste met every DOD and intelligence agency that was launching classified satellites on space shuttle missions, and she was their go-to person who translated what they were going to do, such as deploying their satellites out of the shuttle to begin their DOD mission operations. Much greater communication between DOD and NASA was involved during these missions, since astronauts were now involved in classified missions, and Celeste was in the middle of setting up all these new protocols. While she did this exciting work for a while, she still had this bigger itch to do something with a broader scope—namely, start and run her own business.

But the timing on starting her own business would have to wait. An Air Force colonel introduced her to a man who had started his own business called Scitor, and convinced her to come there. A computer expert, he already had the infrastructure and thought space was cool. Celeste could come in under the Scitor umbrella and "do the space thing." One of the groups already existing at Scitor was preparing to launch a shuttle payload and needed advice. Therefore, she was a perfect fit with them.

Celeste joined Scitor and helped it grow into one of the largest businesses in the industry. After a dozen years of doing that, she was too far removed from "the whites of the customers' eyes," as she puts it. She was receiving plenty of briefings from others but wasn't feeling high personal impact. She certainly had climbed the corporate ladder, but she realized this wasn't how she wanted to spend her time—plus, it wasn't her company. She was successful, but not yet fully in charge. Her next step—and she was always ready for more—was to do exactly what her boss at Scitor had done: start and run her own company.

"I didn't want to be a pest in that regard," she said. "I understood that was the time to start my own business. What I had learned at the third job was the business side. Like, 'Oh, you need a contract, and it needs to be funded.' I feel like between the three experiences—the commercial and international, the defense and intelligence, and now the running of a business—I was ready to strike out on my own."

When Celeste founded Stellar Solutions in 1995, it never occurred to her that she might fail. She knew what was needed and planned to focus on that. Today, her vision hasn't changed, and if you ask any of her two hundred employees, they will tell you that what Celeste has built is not something written on the wall that people must read and believe. Rather, the essence of the company is how its employees live their purpose and mission. It is what they do and how they do it—exactly how Celeste envisioned her business was supposed to be.

Originally, she wanted the company to be small and intimate, no more than fifty people. She had met someone with this criterion for his business and thought that's what she should do—never get so big that she would lose what made it special. She had already been a part of a big firm and saw how you lose focus on high-impact work, taking on pedestrian projects to fit the staff and the business model.

She is quite focused and successful because of it. "We're not going to do that," she said. "Stellar Solutions is stellar, and we are only going to do high-impact work, critical needs—the number-one most critical need, not the tenth—for any customer. To this day, we have a strategic planning process, which started on day one. And almost twenty-five years later, we're still doing it. Every employee uses these criteria. We ask: Is this a critical need for a current customer or a future customer? And if it isn't, we don't include it in our strategic plan or our business plan."

The second component of Celeste's focus is creating dream jobs for her staff, so they feel more like colleagues and teammates. She truly believes and preaches that if you wake up in the morning, love what you do, and know that it's important, it doesn't get better than that. She always thinks the finances are the rearview mirror, a by-product of that alignment of the customer critical need and the right person's dream job. Stellar Solutions employees work hard because they are a services company where they, themselves, are a product. They must be engaged, inspired, and happy so their clients can be as well. Together their work delivers a high impact, and only those individuals who believe that they are special, appreciated, and trusted can deliver on the Stellar promise.

At the beginning, Celeste's goal for the company was to work on all of its projects with this same passion and purpose. As the business grew, it was designed to support an organization that could go on without Celeste, or succession planning. And that is where she believes they are today. Stellar has been listed among *Fortune* magazine's "Great Places to Work" for several years, which is a reflection of her focus and efforts to attract and retain the best people and provide them a business environment in which they can shine. Yet they also know they have to sustain business growth.

In the 2000s, Celeste and Stellar adopted the Baldrige Excellence Framework, which includes "criteria for performance excellence, core values and concepts, and guidelines for evaluating your processes and results." This process gave them tools to enhance their values and core beliefs and build upon their unique culture so they could fully hold themselves accountable. They knew they were doing a lot of wonderful work with customers and employees, but the Baldrige framework gave them something more to model themselves after. The big questions for Celeste and for Stellar were: How would they deploy this model? How would they know if they were walking the talk? What were some benchmark data points? And what were the things they had not done?

As a founder, she realized she was not going to be in charge forever and that more than a gut feeling was needed to ensure that this company could do fine without her. And the Baldrige framework gave them this perspective and purpose with the right metrics, processes, and systems.

For Celeste, winning the Baldrige award represented the crowning glory for her lifelong efforts to push beyond the ordinary into the extraordinary. In May 2018, Stellar Solutions was named a recipient of the Malcolm Baldrige National Quality Award, the nation's highest honor for performance excellence and sustainability. "Receiving the Baldrige Award," they wrote in their press release, "is an incredible honor that recognizes Stellar's sustainability through visionary leadership, organizational alignment, and systemic improvement and innovation," all by a woman-owned small business in the aerospace field.

One of Celeste's biggest concerns about growing her company was that she didn't want to default to what other companies often do when they get larger. As Stellar grew, Celeste flattened the organization and spun out groups so no group had more than twenty people, with a lead identified for each one. The original idea that small is the right size for creative ingenuity and team-building has remained part of her model for building this great company.

As she reflects on her success, Celeste states, "The practice of monthly face-to-face touches with employees and customers is a ground rule, so both stakeholders remain at the core of our communication strategy. If you are the lead of a group, that communications commitment is part of your job. That's the way that we have real-time knowledge. It helps both with the execution of our current projects and informs the way ahead. And then, at the end of the year, we do a big survey and all these questions for both customers and employees to make sure that the monthly talks are really getting at all of the things that we want to know about. So that's our biggest communication strategy—and it does work."

In 2018, I spent a day working with Celeste and her management team to step back and see how a Blue Ocean Strategy might help them open a new market space. As I listened to Celeste tell her story, a lot of ideas came out, trying to connect what I experienced with her team and what her own personal vision was of the type of organization she wanted to create—and had created. Her management team never said those awful words, "That's not how we do it here." Rather, they were hungry for how they could incorporate these new strategies into their organization. They were always looking for unmet needs among their clients. They were thinking about how nonusers could use them. Their new technology for earthquake detection was going to open a new market space that was poorly filled at the time. Stellar was an organization that aspired to set the stage for what could be and how they could lead the field in creating innovative solutions to long-standing problems. They were, indeed, living the "stellar life," and while it is never easy to "live" a brand, Celeste had made her vision come alive.

The word "stellar" is simply a brilliant one to capture the company she envisioned. She wanted everyone to aspire to deliver stellar results and to live a stellar life. The achievement of the Malcom Baldrige award reflected how they had achieved an exceptional organization for both the staff and the customers, all designed and built by a woman smashing through the limits of the aerospace industry.

For Celeste, clients weren't the objects of her actions. They were an integral part of the whole experience, which included how Stellar employees thought about them and engaged with them. Whether it was the Malcolm Baldrige award or recognition in *Fortune* as a great place to work, the echo was acknowledging their culture of caring, concern, and putting the customer first.

From the Observation Deck

Here is where we must step back and look at this story as part of a bigger picture. As you read Celeste Ford's story, you probably wondered how she did it. And perhaps you thought that if she could do it, why aren't there more women in the aerospace world? And most importantly, could you do it as well?

As an anthropologist, I paid attention to the qualities she had that were important to her success. Celeste possesses ingenuity, self-confidence, and a willingness to learn and develop her skills and style along the way. She believed in herself and never seemed to worry about not belonging or not knowing. She is a role model who is contagious, and her company reflects a can-do belief.

Susan Chodakewitz is a woman who is involved in developing women in the aerospace industry. Since 2015, she has been the CEO of Nathan Associates and has also served on the Air Traffic Controllers Association board and the Women in Aerospace board, where she was the chair, among other positions and honors. From her perspective, women are going to have to excel by themselves, developing the technical skills needed by the industry while overcoming the overt and covert biases. There is hope, as the nature of the industry is changing. As Chodakewitz reflects, "I believe that the days of one scientist, or one engineer, or one mathematician—operating in a lab by him or herself—are probably gone. I think that engineering and aerospace are no different than the rest of the marketplace, which requires team interaction, a collective approach to research or development or engineering. And that collaboration, I think, is wonderfully oriented to women, who can bring both the technical and the interpersonal side to the lab."

That means that women are going to have to build those teams and change the culture across the entire ecosystem. They have to be able to talk with potential universities, grad programs, employers—and talk through what the new marketplace looks like. They are going to be transformers without losing focus on the larger problem: namely, how to engage talented women in an industry that needs their creativity and capabilities.

Ironically, demand for talent in the industry is growing exponentially while the supply of talent is shrinking. The 2016 report from the Aerospace Industries Association stressed the serious threat this talent gap poses to productivity, innovation, and competitiveness. In the aerospace and defense sector, the problem is acute. In one study, the association reported that almost 40 percent of aerospace companies predicted an "extreme" impact on their business growth caused by this labor shortage, reflecting concern about not only a lack of senior-level engineers but also a paucity of skilled technical workers versed in technology fundamentals and "soft" skills such as problem-solving, critical thinking, literacy, communication, and collaboration. When we add to this the retiring baby boomers, a major crisis is coming in which women can rise to the top in this industry. The time may be right for young women to see the opportunities surrounding them in aerospace, aviation, and engineering and to apply for them.

That doesn't mean the barrier to entry is gone. Even with the unfilled demand for talented engineers and others, women are going to have to leap over long-held biases and stereotypes, as well as the cultures that continue to reinforce them. It doesn't sound like the industry is going to stretch out and realize it needs those talented women, unless it appreciates what Celeste and other women have done for women and for the industry and embraces them.

Entering a new territory like aerospace might be perfect for you, as a trailblazer and as an individual with great skills and stamina. And something else in Celeste's story should not be lost in our quest to move more women into aerospace careers. The mindset at Stellar is an infectious one. Celeste Ford built a company where men and women wanted to come to work every day. She created a place where people could be themselves and care for their customers in exceptional ways. And she had focus.

Looking back on Celeste's journey, I invite you to think about how you can embody her drive in every aspect of your personal and professional life. Celeste's story is that of someone who didn't see the impossible. Instead, she turned each situation into a building block of possibility for her personal future. And you can too. Boundless opportunities are right before you. Which ones will you pursue?

Women Cannot Rise to Upper Management Roles

"Just don't give up what you're trying to do.
Where there is love and inspiration,
I don't think you can go wrong."

—*Ella Fitzgerald*

Women, how many times have you heard about or watched a woman sitting in a meeting saying something and she was immediately interrupted by a man, discounted by other men, or found a man presenting her ideas as his own? I remember so vividly attending a board meeting at M&T Bank, where I was an executive in one of their divisions. There were forty-nine men and me. I didn't even try to say anything. That feeling of being invisible was a recurring one. For me, as good as I might have been, it seemed to be part of a woman's role, even when I was an executive vice president with a PhD. Perhaps it was always expected that women should be seen but not heard. Women might have ideas, but we were expected to focus on getting them done rather than sharing our opinions. We were raised to let the guys talk and have the last word. What a world to live in for professional women.

That's what Delora Tyler experienced when she worked at the *Detroit News* in the 1970s. It was what propelled her to start her own business and successfully grow it over thirty years, with many male and female clients of various nationalities. They all listened carefully to what she said, because her creative ideas helped them grow their businesses.

Delora was an effective salesperson for the *Detroit News*, bringing in more than $1 million in annual revenues. She built solid relationships with her clients, and many bought full pages of advertising. Yet when Delora would sit in meetings and try to explain to her associates what their customers needed, they refused to listen. They spoke over her. As she said, "They didn't want to hear me." Smart lady as she was, she would whisper to one of her white women coworkers. She would tell her what to say in the meetings, and when that woman said it, the guys would say, "Wonderful. That's a great idea!" to the other woman.

It seemed so strange to Delora that when she started to build her business, her clients—all men—were listening to and trusting her, while her male coworkers at the *Detroit News* had tried to make her disappear. Why was this the case, and why does it continue for so many women? Can women overcome the dynamics and engage with men in ways that allow the women's ideas to be heard and turned into great business value?

You might wonder whether Delora's early challenges stemmed from being an African American or a woman or both. While both presented challenges, she stopped struggling and instead created a different path for herself where the men and the women listened to what she had to say and hired her because of her talent, creativity, and drive. In 1989, after thirteen years at the *Detroit News*, she launched her own company, First Media Group, and after that, nothing stopped her. Now the men were listening.

I met Delora Tyler when I was the interim senior vice president for branding and marketing for a medical center in Michigan, from 2008 to 2012. I knew the CEO at the time, and he had asked me to help him turn around the struggling safety-net hospital. About half of the center's population was African Americans. I knew I needed a marketing agency with talent that understood how to communicate with, mobilize, and engage with this community. I searched for the right agency, and Delora Tyler's name kept coming up.

Delora came over to meet with us, and we quickly got into deep conversations about how to help a hospital and its physicians tackle the healthcare needs of this community.

Delora always laughs at how we bonded so quickly. As we spoke about her own approach to building a marketing campaign, she told me how she would go out into the community and listen. She wanted to know what mattered to the people with whom she was going to have to communicate.

I finally said to her, "You are really an anthropologist at heart, aren't you?" Of course, she understood how observational research could help us both understand the stories people were telling each other about how to get and stay healthy. And Delora could more effectively capture their needs and learn how to engage with them if she spent time listening to their own journeys.

But for Delora to get there, she had to jump over one hurdle after another. I think this quote that is attributed to Reid Hoffman, cofounder of LinkedIn, most definitely describes Delora: "An entrepreneur is someone who will jump off a cliff and assemble an airplane on the way down." To understand Delora's struggles, we should turn to the myth many African American women are still facing in the workplace.

The Myth

Black women in the US face major challenges keeping them from doing great things in business. As you have been reading in our stories, women in general have a hard time breaking through the walls keeping them back. For a black woman, the challenges of both race and gender make it doubly hard. While Delora's first experience with discrimination took place almost fifty years ago, the challenges facing black women today have not changed to the extent we might have wished. Indeed, while we might celebrate the fact that African American women started an average of 541 new businesses per day in the US between 2017 and 2018, we should pause for a moment before we celebrate. The reality is that they are doing it as much out of necessity as to be their own boss or because they have a passion for something. For African American women, the workplaces have not been welcoming. For many of these women, starting their own businesses has been their career survival strategy, as they too realized that the men were not listening.

We might imagine that many black women have been able to overcome these hurdles: Oprah Winfrey, Michelle Obama, or Condoleezza Rice come to mind. Yes, black women have achieved success in the C-suite of major corporations or have become attorneys or accountants or physicians or other business leaders and professionals. But not many. Indeed, black women make up only 2 percent of middle managers in Fortune 500 companies. Ursula Burns, who left the CEO role at Xerox in 2016, is the first and only black woman to occupy the top spot at a Fortune 500 firm.

As of 2015, black women represent 12.7 percent of the US population. Yet they are struggling to move into businesses, professions, and institutions at the degree they should. They have a higher growth rate of college enrollment than any other group and are working in management, professional, and related jobs. While these are impressive advances, black women still face tremendous roadblocks to building income, wealth, and independence.

Compared to white women, black women are less likely to get promoted and are more likely to be pressured to modify their appearance, behavior, and attitudes than white women. Less is expected of them in the professional area, as the myth that black women can only work in supporting roles has been holding them back.

Even the best-trained black women struggle to build careers in large companies. A study of black women MBAs from Harvard Business

School found that with forty years of experience postgraduation, only 13 percent reached senior executive positions, compared with 40 percent of all Harvard MBAs.

Black women attorneys face many of the same limitations. As of 2018, only 4 percent of women attorneys were black. When you look further, the number of black women associates at law firms decreased every year between 2010 and 2015. In 2016, black women made up only 0.64 percent of law firm partners and 2.32 percent of law firm associates.

It is much the same for black women physicians. In 2018, black female doctors represented only 2 percent of the nation's 877,616 active physicians. For those who have persisted and climbed some type of ladder, they have not had an easy time of it. The common theme is they each had more than smarts or luck. But they also were resilient, which is what helped them beat the odds, much like Delora did.

None of this is new or unexpected when set in the context of the deep-seated race and gender discrimination facing black women in the period after the Civil War. The challenges facing black women stem from an entirely white male culture that since the era of slavery has cast them as the "workers." Opening the door for them to move forward, up into business and leadership roles, has not been fast or easy.

On top of this male-dominated workplace culture has been a long, exploitative interaction and dependent relationship between white and black women. Even as we look into the last century, white women were told they were not supposed to work, and many were not even allowed to work. On the other hand, most black women *had* to work. Black women have always made up the highest percentage of women in the labor force, regardless of marital status, education, or number of children in the home. If we look back to 1880, for example, over a third of married black women and two-thirds of single black women worked, while less than 8 percent of married white women and barely a quarter of single white women worked. White women were supposed to take care of the children and the home and, if they could, employ black women for those roles. Unfortunately, not much changed during the twentieth century.

As white women moved into "female jobs" like teaching and nursing, black women were kept down in their educational and professional growth and limited in their career development. Even by 2017, 23.2 percent of black women were still employed in service jobs, compared with 11.6 percent of white women. On the other side, as of 2017, 26 percent of black women held professional positions, compared with 34 percent of white women workers. Black women earn 63 cents for every dollar earned by white male workers, whereas white women workers earn 79 cents for every dollar earned by their male counterparts. For black women, the challenges are particularly overwhelming when 80 percent of them are the breadwinners for their families.

The frustration of trying to build careers in businesses or professions where the rules were defined by white males for white males has led to a mass exodus of black women from the corporate environment into their own businesses. Like Delora, these women decided they could do better on their own. In the decade after the 2008 Great Recession, black women went into their own businesses in record numbers.

How Delora overcame the gender and racial bias and her limited financial assets is a study in endurance, trust, belief in one's self, and a stubborn resistance to "go home again." She was never going to admit defeat, and she was never defeated.

Let's take a look at what Delora was able to achieve and how she did it.

Meet Delora Tyler

Delora is a talented, creative woman who built a successful entrepreneurial business. She was the middle child of four brothers and a sister. Delora grew up in middle-class America in the 1960s. As she jokes, she was born in Henry Ford Hospital, went to Henry Ford High School, and her dad worked for Ford Motors. Her dad was a kind, mild-mannered person, but Delora and her dad had to deal with a firecracker mother who was the disciplinarian in their home. Both her parents wanted their children to go to school. Getting an education was "huge." Once they got it, they were taught that they had to do something with their lives.

Delora's grandmother was always working for more than simply keeping food on the table and the family together. Her grandmother rose above her poverty and raised her daughter, Delora's mother, in a meticulous home. Somehow, everything Delora's grandmother saw in the houses where she worked, she bought for her own home. She wouldn't let her husband drive her all the way to work. He would have to let her out a few blocks away because he was driving a Cadillac. Delora's grandmother didn't want her employers to know she was as well off as they were. She had a beautiful home, a fine wardrobe, and fabulous crystal and china. That's what she did with her money.

Delora's mother was the stay-at-home mom, while her father worked two jobs. When Delora would go school shopping every year, she was the kid who got four pairs of shoes at a time. She was indulged. But one time her mother took back control. Delora's mother had taken her to get a coat that season, and when she got to the store, Delora fell in love with two coats. The second one was soft pumpkin leather and had a white fox collar, and Delora said, "Oh, my God. I've got to have them both."

Her mom said, "OK. Bring them to the counter." When Delora got to the counter with her two special coats, she thought she had really scored that day. She stood dumbfounded when her mother looked at the store owner and said, "Don't you have a job for this kid?" And the lady said, "As a matter of fact, I do." When Delora got in the car, she immediately told her mother that her father wanted her to enjoy her high school life.

Delora reflects, "I knew when we got home, Dad was going to straighten all of this job stuff out." However, that was the day that Delora found out who really ran the family. Delora's mother was setting the stage for Delora to grow up knowing that nothing came easily or only because you wanted it. That following week, Delora was standing in that store saying, "May I help you?" While that was crushing to her at the time, in retrospect, it was one of the best things that could have happened. She adds, "I learned how to communicate with people, how to serve people, and how to be resilient."

Delora has always been fiercely independent. When her mother went to the hospital to have her little brother, Delora was three and a half. She promptly told her aunt that she couldn't wait to get her own apartment because she was tired of her mother telling her what to do. She was all set to take care of herself.

As Delora reflects on her life, she remembers how her mother was on a perpetual roller coaster with her. When people would ask her, "Are you Delora Hall's mother?" she would say, "Why, what did she do?"

When Delora graduated from the University of Detroit in 1977, she had an internship that grew into a job offer. She went to work for the first black-owned television and radio station in the country. She started in programming, and they later allowed her to produce a television show called *Something Special*. She got a chance to learn production, and she loved it. She even got the opportunity to meet some major people.

She knew she needed to learn more and do more, so she left and went to an advertising agency that owned several major record stores back in the day when that was a big business. It was run by an African American family with two sons and was doing quite well. They brought Delora on because they had started their own agency, Progressive Advertising, and wanted her to work there.

Delora started working on major projects, including the first Black Music Month in Detroit. While she was doing interesting things, she wasn't happy with the environment, and so one day on her lunch hour she went down to Channel 4, the NBC affiliate, to apply to be a production assistant. When she was finished, she came out of their offices and looked across the street. There was the *Detroit News*. She figured she might as well go in there and fill out an application as well. While in her mind she was a TV person, she thought she should check to see if there were any opportunities at the newspaper for her. On the application they asked her what job she was applying for, and she said sales, because she knew companies always needed salespeople. She asked for enough money to make it worthwhile, and within a week she was interviewing for a position.

The next thing she knew, she was selling advertising for the fifth-largest newspaper in the country. Delora worked at the *News* for thirteen years, but it was always a combination of pain and pleasure. What she learned was that she had the ability to connect with people. It was her magic sauce. She could sell well because she was focused, responsive, sharp, and never took no for an answer.

As she remembers, "I was selling automotive ads. There was this one man at a dealership that I would go into regularly. Every week I was in there, but he wasn't buying. Finally, he just said, 'Come in here. I just have to give you an ad, because I just can't stand you coming in here every week.'"

Then Delora met Mel Farr, the football player, who had just purchased a car dealership. He would come and sit down with Delora in a small office and work on his ads with her. As Delora remembers it, "I would say, 'Well, you need a quarter page so you can do this.' And he would be like, 'No, I need an eighth of a page.' So we would haggle. He went on to become one of the largest dealers in the country."

He invited her to a dinner event he hosted one time. He had her stand up, and he talked about how he was now buying multiple pages in the paper in full color. He told the audience how she would come in and sit with him and how she worked with him so he could grow his dealership.

Working as an African American female in sales in Detroit, however, was challenging. There was a brick ceiling that wasn't going to let Delora move up, regardless of how successful she was in selling advertising. She was assertive and knew what she was doing. She was more educated than her supervisor and even had to help him spell-check her performance appraisals.

What she did learn was that you needed to know everything about your customers, including how to serve them. She learned the importance of letting them know they mattered. It didn't seem to matter that you were a woman to those clients. If you were selling success, you were great!

The challenge was gaining the respect she felt she deserved within the *Detroit News* organization. When she would go into meetings, she would try to explain, "We need to be doing this for our customers," or "We need to look closer at that." But because of who she was, they couldn't hear her. They didn't want to hear her.

As she watched the dynamics evolve, she realized she wasn't going to do well in that environment. She had grown her territory so large that it would take two people to cover it. Finally, one day they gave her an extra exercise she had to do, where she had to figure out her revenue. Because she was single, she worked differently than her colleagues. When everybody else got off from work to go home, she would go back to sit with her clients—those auto dealers—and even have dinner with them. When she did her calculation, she realized that she was making the *Detroit News* over a million dollars that year. She thought the math was wrong. When she redid everything, her math was right. That's when she said, "You know what, if I can do this for them, then I can do this for me."

When Delora had that realization, she was in her early thirties.

Her insurance agent approached her about creating an advertising campaign for them on the side. Delora decided to moonlight to see what would happen. She worked on his advertising campaign at night, at times burning her dinner because she would forget that she was cooking.

After the campaign launched, she called her client to see how it was going. She kept getting a busy signal. When she finally got through, she said to him, "George, there's something wrong with your phones, because I have been calling all day." His response was "There's nothing wrong with my phones, Delora. This campaign has just been amazing, and I'm going to have to get more phone lines." And then he added, "I want you to be my agency."

That same day Delora went out, picked a name for her new agency, First Media Group, and got it registered. Soon after that on her way into work at the *News*, she looked at the windows and other details in the architecture, because to Delora it was such a big, beautiful, ornate building. As she remembers that day, "I looked at everything. I wanted to remember it, because I said, 'This is my last day.' And I was out." It was 1980.

After she left the *News*, Delora got an opportunity to promote an exhibit at the Detroit Institute of Arts (DIA) that they called "Songs for My People." Within six months, she earned a front-page article for a new client in the *News*, above the fold, which was quite a coup, since she hadn't been allowed to talk to the reporters when she worked there. The exhibit was a major success, and after that Delora said to herself, "OK, let's do this!"

The first year in business was difficult. Her 401k money was her investment to launch the company, and that first year she made only $8,000. The next year, she made $16,000. But First Media kept growing. The third year she made $32,000. It was challenging in the beginning. Delora remembers praying to God and asking what she needed to do to pay her mortgage and keep her car. She says her mother told her, "Well, kid, if it doesn't work out, you can always come home." That motivated her even more. She said she would have worked three jobs if she had to so she wouldn't have to go home. Fortunately, that wasn't necessary.

Delora simply followed her gut. In 1989, when the DIA selected her to promote a special exhibition, she met one of the women who worked there. She recalls, "Cindy had a great personality, and she was just amazing when it came to writing and editing." Delora realized that while she herself was creative, she wasn't a solid writer, so she hired her. Cindy was having her first baby and wanted to work from home. Delora supported that and also found a great graphic artist named Marcina. Her team was virtual at a time when that was unusual. They worked on the phone and the computer. More importantly, they worked well together, understood each other, and built respect collaboratively. These women knew how to focus on the goals and needs of their customers rather than the stature or hierarchy among them.

Her team was racially diverse. And she learned that it was not easy to find and develop talent. Remembering her own travails, she tried to focus on hiring African American interns so she could train them. What she eventually learned was that you have to hire the best people, with the best work ethic, period—even if, as Delora says, "they're polka-dotted." She knew she would only thrive if she hired talented people. Delora was fiercely dedicated and worked around the clock to ensure her work was perfect.

Now, having been in business almost thirty years, Delora is quick to talk about how she grew First Media and what she wishes she knew then. Without realizing it, her business grew through word-of-mouth referrals. Her skills at networking were intuitive and essential. She rarely promoted the company. When she picked up the Michigan Department of Transportation as a client, she was invited to their annual conferences. For five years, she found herself talking to people at these events with little to show for it. Then all of a sudden, her company got an explosion of new business. It had taken five years to build her reputation, and then the referrals kept coming.

As the business grew, she realized that working out of the house was complicated. She was still thinking that her company was a sole proprietorship and that she was working to pay the bills. With large clients coming in, she needed to learn how to run a business and to fund it. While she had stellar credit, in retrospect she should have borrowed as much as she could have because, as she quickly learned, when you need the financing, it is too late to get it. But she managed.

The other thing she began to accept was that she needed the acumen of her husband, whom she had married in 1988. At the time, Donald was working for Conway Transportation. He had a degree in engineering and was an excellent operations manager. He was flying around the country every week. First Media was growing, and he realized that the business required documentation and other things that Delora was unable to deliver, such as reports, analysis, and the cost and benefits of the campaigns. It became clear that it was time for Donald to join Delora to provide the back-office support they both needed if she was going to sleep at night.

Delora was laughing when she recalled their conversations. Donald would ask her about the campaigns. And she would say, "Oh, honey, the campaign was wonderful. The commercial was great." And he would say to her, "Well, what's the ROI on that?" And Delora would say, "ROI? I'm a creative." And he would ask, "Did we make any money?" To which Delora would say, "I think so."

When you are as self-sufficient as Delora, you don't think about what you don't have. In hindsight, she says she should have found mentors. When she finally did, they were invaluable. One, in particular, the head of the Great Lakes Women's Business Council, taught her that at times, she had to fire a client. If a client was difficult or not a good collaborator, Delora realized that her time and effort were never going to work for them. So she learned to say goodbye to those who were unprofitable or difficult to manage.

Delora has also learned to give back to the community. She has been a trustee of the Rosa Parks Scholarship Foundation for more than twenty years. Each year, they select forty graduating high school seniors as their Rosa Parks Scholars and give them $2,000 toward their college education. She was also heavily involved in the Lula Belle Stewart Center for unwed teen mothers who were homeless or had been put out of their homes for being pregnant. The center housed the girls and gave them healthcare while providing daycare for the babies so they could finish their schooling.

As she looks forward, Delora's creativity and desire to share continues to grow. Stay tuned as she plans to unveil a new project promoting entrepreneurship. "This is a great time to be an entrepreneur, especially in Detroit. I hope my concept will help them get more exposure for their businesses by giving them an opportunity to reach a wide, diverse audience." Delora is sure her next project will be a hit—and why not? It is a "Delora" after all, and most everything she touches turns out beautifully.

From the Observation Deck

Now that you've learned about Delora, you may be wondering whether Delora's success stems from how she communicates with others, particularly women but also with men. Did she just hurdle over the standards set by men? And were the men the challenge, or was Delora a headstrong young woman who saw through the rules and wanted to create better solutions? Perhaps all of the above are true. And maybe that is what is needed to completely smash the myth and the roadblocks affecting black women in the workplace.

The continuing problem is that this challenge has not diminished. While it is always hard to know the specifics or the dynamics, Delora was able to take her talents and turn them into a successful entrepreneurial business. While this was thirty years ago, black women like Delora are facing the same issues today—from how to be respected to how to be promoted and listened to.

If we are to smash this myth, we will need to change the perceptions that are creating a false assessment of what women can do, and the standards by which men and women should talk to each other. There is no shortage of stories about women who are breaking down gender barriers today. They really have been for centuries but were never recognized. These trailblazers succeed because of how they work with others. Unlike their male counterparts, these women work collaboratively and with sensitivity while producing amazing business results. Like these women, you too can smash the existing myth about black women in the workplace and capitalize on your own creativity by observing what is around you and coming up with new and innovative solutions.

While Delora has been successful as an entrepreneur, her success was early in the development of women entrepreneurs from the African American community. Today, African American women present a very different story. For black women, the possibilities that entrepreneurship offers are expanding exponentially. According to American Express's *2018 State of Women-Owned Business Report*, while the number of women-owned businesses grew an impressive 58 percent from 2007 to 2018, the number of firms owned by black women grew by 164 percent, nearly three times that rate. There are 2.4 million African American women-owned businesses in 2018, most owned by women ages thirty-five to fifty-four. Black women are the only racial or ethnic group with more business ownership than their male peers. Among the biggest challenges for these women is that African American women have to build their companies, as Dell Gines, the author of *Black Women Business StartUp*, says, "with only a toothpick and a napkin."

It is not surprising, however, that the major reasons black women are going into their own businesses is that they are struggling inside companies to find the type of positions, salaries, and respect they deserve. Much like Delora, black women are frustrated on the job, passed over for promotions, and experience workplace exhaustion and hierarchies that are immoveable. Unfortunately, the same brick ceiling exists today for black women as it did thirty years ago.

Now that Delora has found success, she wants to help these women. Part of her drive and passion is her desire for women to understand that they are smarter than others think they are. She wants you to know that you're stronger than you imagine and that it is time to stop letting men define you. Like Delora, African American women entrepreneurs must be more self-confident and build their resilience.

To smash this myth, you have to believe in yourself and keep pushing forward. If Delora were here right now, she would tell you to "go get it." When you stop letting things hold you back and think, "Yes, you can," you will discover, like Delora, that you can too!

Women Don't Belong in IT

"Instead of thinking out of the box,
get rid of the box."

—*Deepak Chopra*

When I met Samantha Radocchia (she goes by Sam Rad), I knew I had a myth-smasher. Sam was presenting at a Crain's conference, speaking about blockchain and the future of supply chains and of everything else that is changing in the ways we work, eat, live, and manufacture goods. She was commanding my undivided attention, because I'm a blockchain voyeur. I am not sure how it might affect me, but I am sure blockchain is going to change the world as we know it today.

I had done several podcasts with DigiByte founder Jared Tate. I'd also interviewed Marten Ven from Te Farms in Germany on their blockchain expansion and watched as Walmart was asking food vendors to put blockchain on their lettuce to ensure it was what had been ordered. Even the city of Zug, Switzerland, was putting all of its residents' identities, tax returns, and other valuable data onto blockchain. And here was Sam talking about her company, Chronicled, that was developing highly secure blockchain systems for the supply chain world.

She was talking about her own experiences, and I was watching the power and presence of the next generation of women in tech right before me. Sam was not just a coder, although she had taught herself to code at the age of twelve, building video games and websites about puppies after having gone to a website-building camp with her brothers.

During our conversation, I discovered that Sam is much more than an engineer. She had studied anthropology through graduate school, focusing on technology's impacts on society. Before that, she had attended film school and worked extensively in theater—a skill that was obvious by her stage presence and charisma. In fact, Sam really did not have a category or a box to fit into. She was a brilliant creator. She was less concerned with how the code was created than with what could be done with the systems and software to change how we did things. Sam wanted to know how these new systems impacted society and wanted to find ways to make our lives work—and most importantly, feel—better. She aimed to use technology to empower, not entrench—to restore connections between people and themselves, people and each other, people and the environment, and people and the products they consumed. Hers was an idealistic promise that the web 2.0 technologies of years past had failed to deliver on.

As I listened to her talk, I became excited to share her story. She had already been ranked by *Forbes* in the 2017 *Forbes* 30 Under 30. I wanted to know who Sam was and why she was ignoring the barriers for women in technology. Instead of trying to fit into the IT world, she was creating a new world, educating a society, and showing a way forward to other women.

The Myth

First, let's take a look at the stories around women and IT, and even around science, technology, engineering, and mathematics—all those letters in STEM. The reality is that women are simply not going into IT as often as men. They are going into some fields of science, such as the biological sciences, social sciences, and psychology. These are fields where women make up over 54 percent of the bachelor's degrees and 57 percent of the doctorate degrees. Women are also strong in math. They have 42 percent of the bachelor's math degrees and 41 percent of the master's math degrees. In computer sciences, however, women have only 18 percent of the bachelor's degrees, 30 percent of the master's degrees, and 20 percent of the doctorate degrees. In engineering, there are even fewer women.

There is no shortage of research and mythmaking about why women are not in these fields to the degree that people think they should be. Some think this is a problem because of the personal computer, which replaced the desktop and resulted in boys having access to video games, which led to them learning to code with greater facility and positive reinforcement than girls. Others claim that boys pushed girls away from the computers, because boys seemed to be able to solve computer problems faster than their female counterparts. Still others are sure it is because the entire coding process is counter to what girls enjoy—it lacks certainty and requires ingenuity to solve complex programming problems. And there are those who believe girls and women prefer reading to the sciences, even though they score equally with the boys and the men on those science skills.

Perhaps it is because young women see few women going into STEM careers, so they have fewer role models and don't define these as female careers and seek other avenues that are deemed more feminine. The thinking continues that women in science success stories are not frequently shared or celebrated, thus diminishing their value and significance. In fact, in 2019 a physicist, Jess Wade, wrote more than 280 Wikipedia pages to showcase another group besides white men in science. Wade wrote up a large group of women scientists into Wikipedia, because they were all missing from the online encyclopedia.

Then there is the rampant or subtle sexism in the workplace. Because those workspaces are dominated by men, they create an environment where women feel unwanted, as they are deemed outsiders in a male-defined culture. The lack of women in leadership roles in these organizations only underscores this.

Among the most interesting research was conducted by Kugler, Tinsley, and Ukhaneva and published in Vox in November of 2017. They attempted to systematically evaluate the experiences of men and women in a large private university. They wanted to capture data about why women and men went into certain majors and either stayed in them or changed their majors, all the while searching for what influenced women and their career choices. What they found was that women were getting multiple signals that they did not fit in the STEM majors.

Ironically, during the early years of computing and computer science, when the fields of computer sciences, IT, and STEM were less controlled by men and not yet well-structured, women were extremely important in the design and development of computers and in the early period of software system creation, and even coding.

Think about the genius of some of these women. They were crafting entirely new fields. In the late 1800s, Williamina Fleming, a housekeeper for Edward Pickering, the head of the Harvard College Observatory, was asked by Pickering to do a job that the men at the observatory refused to consider—analyzing the data that those men were collecting from their telescopes. She worked literally as a "computer" to compile the data and make it understandable, ultimately building a team of more than eighty women to become Harvard's "computers."

By the beginning of the twentieth century, these Harvard computers grew into a group of women mathematicians at NASA and its Jet Propulsion Laboratory. During World War II, these women did all the calculations to plot the ballistic trajectories and build the programming for the ENIAC computer. Six of these women became the world's first coders, manipulating the ENIAC to calculate missile trajectories.

Other women who were innovators in the field included Grace Hopper, who, after working at the Harvard Computational Lab, was transferred to Eckert-Mauchly Computer Corp., where she helped develop the UNIVAC I computer in 1949. She became known as "Amazing Grace" and "the first lady of software." Her focus was to make coding languages more practical and accessible. By translating source code from one language to another, Hopper was thinking well beyond what was in place. These were big ideas at the time and fundamental to setting up what was to come next.

As I researched the many women who were creating this new field, I loved reading about Anne Easley. Easley, an African American, had read an article about twin sisters who were "human computers" at the Aircraft Engine Research Laboratory in Ohio. The lab was looking for people who had strong mathematical and analytical skills. Easley was looking for a job and found a home there. In 1955, Easley began her career as a human computer, doing computations for researchers. For thirty-four years she worked at what was to become the NASA Glenn Research Center. Easley was one of four African American employees at NASA at that time. As human computers were replaced, Easley learned to re-skill herself and became a highly competent computer programmer. Some of her legacy was the work she did researching energy-conversion systems, including the battery technology used for early hybrid vehicles.

And many do not know that it was Mary Allen Wilkes who helped develop the first "personal computer." She also is thought to be the first person to have had a computer in her home. Wilkes is credited with writing the LINC's operating program manual. Her quote is a reflection of the challenges facing everyone in the field: "We had the quaint notion at the time that software should be completely, absolutely free of bugs. Unfortunately, it's a notion that never really quite caught on."

Then there was Adele Goldberg, the only woman on a team of men building the Smalltalk-80 programming language and later the design to the Windows display screen, or Graphical User Interface (GUI). One of the most respected people at that time in the software industry, she worked for the Xerox Palo Alto Research Center. She was the cofounder of ParcPlace-Digitalk, producing application development environments for software developers. Her work on Smalltalk became the foundation for WIMP (windows, icons, menus, pointers) that were the foundation for today's user interfaces.

Donna Dubinsky introduced the "personal digital assistant," which was the foundation of the Palm Pilot. If you ever had one, it was quite remarkable. Dubinsky, a Harvard Business School alumna and a former Apple employee, built the first PDA company, Palm. Following Palm, she created Handspring, which was able to store data and access programs beyond the calendar.

And Megan Smith is credited with helping bring the US government beyond its floppy disks when she worked with President Barack Obama. She advised him on keeping the internet open and free and worked to bring women into science and technology.

The list continues and is quite long and impressive. Women have been playing major roles in the origins of modern computing and systems and their design and applications for the kinds of uses we have today. In many other countries, women are on par with men in their training, development, and participation in STEM. However, over 70 percent of the researchers in science are men. Only 20 percent of the countries have close to gender parity where women are close to 50 percent of the science researchers. Women were clever, creative, and successful in computers, programming, and STEM before today. So why the decline? The world of IT was not making them want to join and stay. Women were not encouraged to pursue careers in these fields, and when they did, they felt like outsiders, so many of them left.

Fortunately, today in areas of emerging technologies—such as blockchain, artificial intelligence, and quantum computing—there are women who are building systems to facilitate financial transactions, others who are working on cryptocurrency, and more who are developing cross-border credit-scoring platforms. If we look at the themes from before, where women shined, they were innovators and early adopters. These women were creatives; they created the codes when the men didn't think it worthy to do computational work. They saw things through a fresh lens during a time of change. They made things happen, often as part of a team of other men and women. They were clever and creative and even willing to be different.

I was starting to think that maybe the field of computer science was the problem and not the women who didn't want to code or become computer engineers. Could someone like Sam Radocchia shed some light on the type of woman who could help the STEM world? And could she help us understand how these types of women might be great role models for other women who could see problems to solve and help find creative solutions for them in the IT industry? I was fascinated by this possibility and couldn't wait to talk with Sam to learn more.

Meet Samantha Radocchia

Sam is a serial entrepreneur working mostly with emerging and deep tech, as well as an author, keynote speaker, and technology advocate. When you meet her, you are sure she has some magic secret that you just have to have. She is an organizational anthropologist (but likes to call herself a cultural technologist, combining the fields of anthropology and technology) and has successfully combined her interest in people, their myths, and their languages with the training and interests of a scientist. She also has the charisma of a leader who can speak with audiences at all levels about their fears and embracing change with an abundance mindset, converting her passion for technology and change into a belief that they, too, can aspire to great things in this emerging new world. While she never talks about the Fourth Industrial Revolution, straying away from the use of buzzwords, Sam is indeed an early product of an entirely new world that is emerging fast and changing everything.

Sam grew up in a family that had a prosperous retail business. She and her brothers often hung out in the warehouse, watching the systems and the business run. Growing up with brothers, she was quite a video gamer. Today, she calls herself a "reformed" gamer. Ever the adventurer, before heading off to college, she took a gap year, got her pilot's license, went to film school, and started her passion for skydiving. By 2020, Sam had done over seven hundred competitive jumps.

She went to Colgate University from 2007 to 2011. Sam had enough credits from her summer studies to graduate from film school in 2010. At Colgate, Sam studied anthropology, linguistics, and theater. She chose anthropology because after a brief stint with neuroscience, she realized anthropology was the best lens to view her varied interests, which ranged from human societies and behavior to linguistics, English, and theater. She had done quite a bit of acting growing up and loved to perform, organize, and live in the world of theatrical productions. Sam found her calling in directing, enjoying working with the most comprehensive of mediums—human beings and human emotions. While she was there, she started a theater company in the town of Hamilton, where the college was located. She would write and direct and put on plays with people in town, mostly with older adults in the local community. Sam loved helping people bring out their true selves—usually it was older folks who always wanted to be in theater performing for the first time. But she never asked if she could start a company. She just did it.

Sam has always been fascinated with technology. She started studying virtual currencies in 2009 while writing her anthropology thesis on currency exchanges in the virtual world "Second Life." She was digging deeper into all of the things that fascinated her while they also set up a platform for her to discover things that might be buried in current mythology.

This was right after the 2008 recession hit. Although she graduated magna cum laude with a BA in English and anthropology, Sam knew that finding a job as an anthropologist or a theater director was not going to happen. Instead, being Sam, she decided to start her own company. She was watching folks turn on their computers and shop online during class. While she watched, she wondered why people were aimlessly scrolling down the pages. So she decided to build an algorithm like Pandora's AI-powered recommendation application. There wasn't an app then, because phones weren't widespread for people to shop on at the time. What Sam wanted to create was a method for capturing people's tastes and then offering them recommendations on products, based on their preferences.

That summer, Sam corralled her brother and some of his friends into working with her in her Brooklyn loft, instead of taking internships at Google or Apple. Her brother and his roommates were all in STEM or computer science at the University of Pennsylvania. She gathered them together to build a "bunch of stuff," as she refers to it. During their venture Sam filmed the entire experience, figuring she could make a documentary of how they were spending the summer during a recession.

A friend of theirs pitched the raw video footage to a major television network, which picked up the option for a reality TV show. In a whirlwind experience of events, what started as a project was now a company that was being filmed 24/7 by professional directors who had shot Oscar-winning films. Sam's company was suddenly pitching to major Fortune 100 brands and onboarding tens of thousands of customers seemingly overnight. Somewhere in between, Sam heard the network was going to sell the option to a less-than-ideal network and turn the show into a more drama-focused reality TV show, so she purchased the rights—a savvy contract negotiation for the then twenty-two-year-old founder.

She had originally expected to have a three-month fun summer project, and it somehow became "real" while they were building all types of systems to solve real computer problems. Before long, after the whirlwind dance with network TV, however, Sam realized that she had to rethink. Someone had to step up and monetize this venture as she continued to build a system that could sell everything by integrating inventory in real time from all the different e-commerce sites.

This was an early application program interface (API)—a set of routines, protocols, and tools for building software applications—which is now common language. At the time, however, it was unique. Half of their business was consulting, as they built these structures for people, and half of their business entailed integrating the systems of inventory and payments. As she reflects on her first business, she says, "I don't know how I did this. I was super naïve. I didn't have the technical knowledge at the time, and I think that was exactly why I was able to do it." Her timing was a little early, and today all types of companies are doing this. At the time, people kept saying to her, "That's impossible. How did you do that?" From Sam's perspective, she was able to be bold and creative because she didn't know she couldn't do it. She and her team just did it, and it worked.

When she realized that growth was limited, she sold the front-end AI part of the business and kept the systems integration part. While she had some idea that she might build a business around it, it didn't materialize until later in her career, when she discovered blockchain.

In June of 2011, she formed Machine Elf Consulting—since rebranded to Radical Next—as a new style of business advisement and consultancy services. She geared her focus toward enterprises,

C-suite, and board-level executives, institutions, analysts, and start-ups that wanted to understand and leverage exponential technologies such as blockchain, internet of things (IoT), artificial intelligence (AI), machine learning, and additive manufacturing. Their inter-disciplinary approach synthesized traditional product development, marketing, and managerial guidance with innovative strategies.

While she was running her first company, she was also working on her master's degree at King's College London, where she studied management and entrepreneurship, and the London School of Eco-nomics, where she studied organizational culture. She ended up going back to New York because of the growth of the first company and then graduated from New York University summa cum laude in the spring of 2013 with an MA in media, culture, and communications, with a focus on the sociopolitical analysis of emerging technologies.

Around that time Sam realized she needed some coding skills, so she took a coding boot camp while she was consulting. Then she moved out to the West Coast and on to Park City, Utah, where she got her EMT license and became a ski patroller. At the same time, she was still doing consulting as well as building software products and software teams. Out of these consulting projects, her next company emerged. This one came out of her serendipitous meeting with a man while she was in Park City. He was the youngest board member of Overstock.com. He had left the company to start his own. He was all of thirty-one and wanted to create a loyalty product. Sam joined him and got back into bitcoin and cryptocurrencies. She built the first product herself and then hired an extended remote engineering team. She cofounded the company as the chief technology officer (CTO). This was a short stint of a year as she learned the differences of being a consultant and building a company again where she was not the solo founder.

Around that time, she was getting into the community of block-chain and met her cofounders of Chronicled, who came together on various internet platforms. They collectively came up with an idea to explore the technology, and together they thought they could build it into a company. A private equity fund had hired a CEO who was working on his concept when his path crossed with Sam's. Chronicled turned into a five-year experience for Sam.

Based in San Francisco, Chronicled is a software technology company leveraging blockchain to bring trust, efficiency, and automation to global supply chain ecosystems. The company has developed tools and protocols to enable decentralized blockchain networks that support multiparty supply chain workflows, enabling enterprises to extend trust boundaries and enforce cross-organization business rules without revealing private data. Their customers range from Fortune 50 pharmaceutical, commodities, and chemical companies—a significant expansion from Chronicled's early days of serving the luxury goods, precious metals, and CPG markets.

Today, Sam has an impressive list of accomplishments. She made the 2017 *Forbes* 30 Under 30 List for Enterprise Technology. She also has been a strong advocate of blockchain and wrote a book titled *Bitcoin Pizza: The No-Bullshit Guide to Blockchain*, which examines the cultural history of the technology and the impacts of decentralization on the world today, tomorrow, and the near future. Sam speaks around the globe on blockchain, artificial intelligence and machine learning, quantum computing, and other emerging technologies, along with the future of work and of our decentralized society. Sam notices how everything from finances, education, healthcare, supply chains and manufacturing, and food production are radically changing. In founding several companies and serving as a CEO, as well as leading product and engineering teams as both a CTO and chief product officer (CPO) and leading marketing teams as a chief marketing officer (CMO), Sam is an avid creator of intellectual property and holds several patents. She was an early outspoken voice in blockchain as the cofounder of Chronicled.

Personally fascinated with the future of work, remote first teams, and distributed or decentralized organizations, she is trained in and speaks on organizational culture and theory. Her lectures on technology, risk, abundance versus fear-based mindsets, emotional intelligence, and intuition have been featured by globally recognized universities such as MIT, Columbia, Harvard, and University College London, national governments, Fortune 500 companies, and institutions such as the United Nations.

Sam has already created a remarkable legacy, all before her early thirties. She has built experimental cities, leveraging blockchain, IoT, robotics, and AI. She has also assisted in the creation of large-scale role-playing games (RPG) and virtual world architecture. Sam has deployed mesh sensor networks across small- and medium-sized cities and worked with governments to track temperatures of volatile substances and medicines across hostile environments. She has rolled out identity and cryptocurrency to disaster zones and refugee camps and architected a decentralized manufacturing network with connected 3D printers and 3D knitters. She has even deployed a drone delivery and authentication service on blockchain; has assisted in the creation of a smart charging station for autonomous vehicles; and somehow finds the time to write about all of this in her blog, Radical Next Ideas with Sam Rad.

But Sam is so much more than a list of accomplishments or an impressive legacy. As you speak with her, you realize that she sees the bigger picture of what is happening in the world, way beyond any one company. She has a deep passion to understand and explain to others the future of society, which encompasses the future of not only work but food, housing, healthcare, education, and supply chains/manufacturing, including how production and distribution will evolve with the new technologies that are here today. When you see it all coming together as she does, you know that the world of work as we know it is going to be transformed—quickly—and probably before we are ready to adapt to it. And once you realize that you need to understand the world around you and that you need to understand the people's needs in that world, then and only then will you know what exactly you should be building to anticipate and solve problems. All this happens long before you start designing, developing, and coding systems.

From the Observation Deck

We began this chapter by raising the myth that women do not belong in the IT industry and then began to explore why women haven't gravitated toward careers in coding and computer science. We learned that part of it is that women do not feel welcome in this male-dominated space. But more importantly, women appear to be choosing what capitalizes on their creative, collaborative capabilities instead. Like Sam, they see the bigger picture surrounding these technological changes and are asking different questions about how they can help solve the world's—or even their own—challenges.

When speaking with Sam, I noticed that she didn't refer to herself as someone in IT. She isn't even sure what that means anymore. She also isn't thinking outside of the box. Instead, she is creating an entirely new box to explore and share with others. And most importantly, she has been so successful in the tech field because she has found her passion, which fuels and sustains her belief that she can do whatever it is that she wants to achieve.

All of this hasn't come without hardships for Sam, however. She notes times where others have not quite grasped the boxes she was creating for herself, noting, "I can't tell you how many times people have told me 'You are the most exceptional person I have ever met, but you aren't a deep vertical chief marketing officer' or 'You're by far the most intuitive futurist I have met, but you're not a venture capitalist.'" She's recently accepted that perhaps she represents a new class of entrepreneurs, founders, and builders that exist beyond traditional titles and boxes. For now, her generalist horizontal management style places her in the CEO role, but perhaps in the future even that will change as companies evolve to become more flat and distributed.

Her story is an important one to share. She has a deep concern for the changes taking place in our society and the culture that supports it. While she is trying to find a place where she feels most at home, she is also traveling the world, working from wherever she is, and speaking to whomever wants to know more about the technological transformation of what is called the Fourth Industrial Revolution.

Perhaps it is her fresh perspective that reminded me of all of those highly talented women before her who were the computers at Harvard or who worked on the UNIVAC or did the programming for the bombers in the Second World War. Sam Rad is opening up an entirely new market space—and it isn't only in coding. It is in the intersection of all of these areas, from blockchain to AI to 3D printing and autonomous vehicles to cryptocurrency and new supply chains. Hers is the new world that she is helping to create, without corporate boundaries or national borders.

As we think about what Sam Rad has done, we must ask what this great technological transformation will do for men and women, and women in particular, in the near future. Will the Fourth Industrial Revolution build better equity between men and women or worsen it? Whose brains are going to be best suited for what comes next, women's or men's? As more and more systems and processes become automated and systematized, how will we nurture the creative, left-brain thinkers and organizations that don't quite fit in the boxes of yesteryear?

Only when women and men collaborate and integrate their work will the next revolution transform society in ways that are more positive, productive, and full of possibilities for people at all levels in our societies and across the globe. The coming changes and the speed of them are going to require a great deal of re-skilling of adults and new ways of learning for young children. Efforts to foster a world where girls and boys learn and love STEM and how they can apply it innovatively and creatively are going to be essential.

The work of Youth for Technology Foundation (YTF) is one organization that has a highly innovative and effective approach to bring technology and entrepreneurship to young people, particularly to women across the globe. Their focus is on careers where women can offer great value and not find themselves automated out of a job. But their concern is as valid for boys and men as it is for women. Manufacturing, construction, and even farming (which are today mostly male-dominated industries) will be facing massive transformations as robots replace humans, and self-driving tractors and drones supplant human labor. Even healthcare is going to be facing great changes as technology supplants human physicians, a number of doctors and nurses age out of place, and the percentage of women in the field eclipses men.

Women, ironically, have the agility, creativity, and ability to navigate these changes. Much as Sam has done, they can take their learning and creative mindsets and use a collaborative approach to problem-solving to find a path where they can be of great value in the new world that is here today. Those "softer" skills that enhance communication and coordination are going to be the ones that we will need to thrive in these fast-changing times.

We might not realize it, but change is all around us. Since we know that our brains hate to change, we must turn to people like Sam to lead the way. All industrial revolutions emerge and surge as a result of the choices people make, individually or together. It is well beyond the ideas of the creators. It is how these ideas are turned from innovative to ubiquitous, such as blockchain becoming a way to use a new currency to buy pizza and to organize a supply chain where you can track and trace where your food has come from.

Those of us who are willing to smash the prevailing myth about women entering the IT and computer sciences field are the ones who are going to envision a future where women coders are programming and turning these new technological possibilities into realities. None of Sam's innovations have come from any basement or garage, where she sat alone mulling over new ideas. Each innovation came from gathering others together and thinking about building a new reality. There is power in collaboration. Just as Sam did when she began studying virtual currencies and their applications, I invite each of you to gather your own team where you can work with other innovators to participate in this Fourth Industrial Revolution as you build the future of your dreams.

Anthropologists Don't Work in Business

"We are all faced with a series of great opportunities
brilliantly disguised as impossible situations."

—Charles R. Swindoll

As you've been reading these stories, you may have been wondering
what my story was and if I, too, had to smash any myths. As I was
writing this book, I kept wondering why it was so important to
me to share these myths and stories with others. I also wondered
if these women who were opening up new paths for others were
simultaneously telling me something about what I had done in the
field of applied or corporate anthropology. After writing these stories, the time seemed right to reflect on my own journey and see
how it could shed light on the ways in which the social sciences,
particularly anthropology, had to change to survive and thrive in
this century.

As I was completing my doctoral training in the early 1970s, it was
quite clear that anthropologists were rarely employed in or working
with businesses. For me, employment in business was the last thing
on my mind. I was already working at an interdisciplinary college,
Ramapo College in New Jersey, and I was in a tenure-track position.
This was what I was anticipating, and it all seemed so easy.

Today, many claim that anthropology is the worst major to take in college. People say few business jobs are out there for them. I think this is more about the business community not knowing much about the social sciences or anthropology than the limits of anthropology itself.

Anthropologists are of great value to corporations. They are often hired to help businesses that are stuck or wanting to grow to see things with fresh eyes. SteelCase has used anthropologists to better understand how people use space so they can design appropriate workspaces. Ford routinely hires anthropologists to study their showrooms, bringing their executives into the reality of car sales and improving their marketing messages. Intel has also hired dozens of anthropologists who work closely with their software engineers and with the end-users of their technology. Microsoft is one of the largest employers of anthropologists, hoping their perspectives and observations can improve the products and services designed for different types of organizations. The list continues to grow of large and small companies using anthropologists.

When I launched my consulting firm in 2002, after twenty years in business with executive positions, my PR guru, John Rosica, said, "Andi, you are a corporate anthropologist who helps companies change." This one-sentence elevator speech captured exactly who I was and what I wanted to do. If you did a Google search at that time, I doubt there were a dozen people looking for a corporate or business anthropologist. Yet clients came to us because they wanted or needed to change—and they came quickly.

People said, "I thought an anthropologist was a person like Margaret Mead who studied small, exotic cultures." Well, perhaps businesses are small, exotic cultures. They need anthropologists to help them see what is actually taking place both inside their organizations and around them. We are a mashup of *Undercover Boss* and a participant observer hanging out to listen and watch, learning what is important and how people get through their daily lives. This is as relevant to understanding customers and noncustomers as it is to capturing the workplace culture.

Some of the stories in my award-winning book *On the Brink: A Fresh Lens to Take Your Business to New Heights*, came out of the work I did with companies that needed a new perspective. Each of the case studies were of companies that were stalled or stuck and needed my firm to step in and help them see what was all around them. Once they did, they restarted their engines and soared.

Today, my consulting firm is growing, and I have never looked back. I hope by sharing my journey from academia, through corporate executive positions, and into my own corporate anthropology consulting firm will help all the anthropologists who are looking to apply their own work in the business arena.

It turns out that, like many of the other women in this book, I had to smash a myth to do my own thing. Later, you will learn how I became a corporate anthropologist in a territory where most academics in the societal sciences dared not tread. By reading my story, you will see how anthropologists, and those who are willing to look at the world through a fresh lens, can create new ways to add value to businesses, industries, and society.

The Myth

Research by the National Science Foundation found that in 2013, about 14 percent of anthropologists held private sector jobs. Most anthropology students were being groomed for academic positions. Yet there were few, if any, academic tenure-track jobs for anthropologists. The research estimate is that 79 percent of US anthropology doctorates do not have tenure-track positions in US institutions.

Further, since 1993, college faculty do not have to retire, ever. As a result, the number of job openings for tenure-track positions, or really for any positions, has made anthropology the worst major of any in the US. Yet colleges and universities continue to turn out graduates with the illusion that they are being prepared for academic positions.

What is wrong with this picture?

First, the faculty at these universities and colleges have one mission: to train students for jobs like theirs. They are creating too much supply without ever creating new demand. They have their tenure and their perception of reality, but it isn't a good reflection of what is out there for their students. The faculty are convinced that their job is to train the next generation of professional anthropologists who are going to seek tenure-track positions and do research. In short, they are selling hope!

Second, some institutions recruit students into their colleges or universities without considering what to do to help them when they leave. We have worked with several higher education institutions, and we continue to tell them that their real job is to find jobs for their students well before they graduate. These higher education institutions should become the placement officers for the industries that are turning to them for their future staff. During these fast-changing times, that role is of even greater importance, because their graduates should continue to come back for re-skilling throughout their lives as the times continue to change. We are in the midst of the Fourth Industrial Revolution, and it is transforming the way each of us works.

Then there are the businesses, industries, and their leadership, many of whom have no idea what a social scientist or an anthropologist could do with them or for them. Think about the range of jobs to be done inside a company where an anthropological perspective would be of great value: from building a strong culture to enabling business leaders to better understand their current customers, future customers, and even their own employees.

Often, one of the problems is that business leaders don't know how to talk to academic anthropologists. Consequently, conversations sound as if there are two foreigners in need of a translator, mostly around the cultural meaning of the words of those conversations. The talk is typically all about what "I" do, not what "we" can do together. Further, as I learned when I worked in industry, business is about business. Unless an academic can demonstrate competency in business, they don't have the credibility needed to advise others.

Last, there are the students and their parents. Anthropology majors are being taught great theories, methods, and tools. They go on field trips to learn how to step back, observe societies all across the globe, and help better understand what they do and how they do it. Yet they are inside their own anthropological culture. Ironically, they are not looking at their own culture as an anthropologist should, with dispassionate attention to the nuances, practices, stories told, and mythologies being shared, affirmed, and protected.

The conversations, as at one societal meeting of professional applied anthropologists, was about how the CEO in a client company did not accept their recommendations. In fact, the anthropologist mourned that the CEO and his C-suite discounted much of what they had observed and reported on. Another young man told me how he did user experience anthropological work inside a large bank. Instead of benefitting from his observations and research, he was the "box they checked off," as they seemed to discard his findings. It's almost as if these anthropologists were seen as a set of barbarians, challenging the truths that these businesses believed to be their reality. These businesses were unable to appreciate the services they had contracted these anthropologists to do.

Today there are some exciting companies and individuals doing anthropology in business. Their approaches are innovative, and their methodologies are insightful. The way they interact with companies has opened up new avenues for ethnographic research and trained new anthropologists. I am particularly impressed with the work of Rita Denny. Her consulting firm, Practica Group, has a team of anthropologists, social scientists, psychologists, technologists, medical anthropologists, and sociolinguists who are amplified when needed by experts. They work with a wide range of industries, often around their marketing and their markets. Rita specializes in helping companies better utilize ethnographic research with a focus on conversations and the new insights that linguistics can provide into what people mean when they share their stories and converse in social interactions. Her award-winning books, coauthored and coedited with Patricia Sunderland—*Doing Anthropology in Consumer Research* and *The Handbook of Anthropology in Business*—captured the wide range of applied anthropology being done in businesses or for them.

Some of the work is on the cutting edge of how anthropological methods can shed fresh perspectives. Many companies are now hiring anthropologists. Google, for example, has hired a number of ethnographers to study how people use mobility and mobile devices. And then there's Steelcase, with their ownership of IDEO, which truly understands the value of ethnographic research in the entire design process. When James Hackett acquired IDEO, he understood how design thinking needed an observational component to better understand the customer and the problem to be solved.

When Hackett later became head of Ford Motors, he brought in anthropologists to take executives out into the field to better understand how customers used their showrooms and their automobiles. Ford became interested in how vehicles affect human lives. And Michael Thomas, a cultural anthropologist, has been working to improve Ford's marketing strategies by better understanding the consumer and their feelings about the cars they buy.

Intel has written a great deal about how Genevieve Bell, their in-house cultural anthropologist, together with the over one hundred researchers she manages, studies how people interact with electronics. Some of her work in China was converted into a new computer strategy to target Chinese parents and their children. Bell was an important part of Intel's idea development and technology innovations. Her role was to help Intel's chipmakers power new devices, develop new software, and expand their markets by helping their technologists see how people would use their technology in daily life. Stephen Pawlowski, the head of research at Intel, states, "Genevieve and her team cause us engineers to think differently. We intend to use Bell's expertise heavily as we focus on emerging growth markets."

What customers want from a product and what companies think they want can be totally different, but it can take an anthropological lens to learn why. The oft-cited story is about how ReD Associates used anthropological methods to help Adidas discover that yoga was a sport, and with their insights helped the company reposition itself to a much wider audience than just the serious athletes of the past. ReD has for many years helped companies, large and small, realize they have been getting humans all wrong. They know how to use the human sciences to observe people and open the minds of the businesses to what people actually do, think, and feel, rather than just what the business thinks.

You may be wondering: If anthropologists can help companies see things through a fresh lens, why aren't more companies hiring them? And how can an anthropologist step back and see themselves in a new way—as someone primed to join a company to help them grow? Read on to learn how I smashed the predominant myth, opening the door for others to follow.

Let Me Share My Story

If anthropology is truly the worst major, then we, as anthropologists, have a mission to transform the benefits of an anthropological degree into a new reality, with new stories to support the work that anthropologists can do.

It's true that I have rarely been hired because I was an anthropologist. Rather, organizations hired me to help them change—whether it was Citibank or Poughkeepsie Savings Bank, Montefiore Medical Center or St. Joseph's Regional Medical Center. The clients in my firm typically came to me when they were at the end of their own creative ideas and needed a new way to think about their organization and its future. My colleagues and I often served as the metaphorical fire department when we were finally called in to help.

Yet we had become a busy consulting firm. We defined ourselves as corporate anthropologists to help organizations that needed or wanted to change. Knowing that humans hate to change, we set ourselves up to fail. Who would hire us to help them do what their brains hated to do?

But as we launched our business in 2002, we had a steady stream of clients from Marcal Paper and Montefiore Medical Center to Centenary College and Atlantic Health System, and many others. It didn't matter the type of company or industry. They all needed a fresh approach to address their challenges. We learned as we grew that we could help others turn their own anthropological skills into new opportunities. With each client we discovered that businesses need anthropologists. They just needed to know what anthropologists did. Once we showed them how to see in new ways and how they could work to change their way of seeing and doing with creative and effective results, they saw the inherent value in our work, and word began to spread.

Before I became a corporate anthropologist or even a cultural anthropologist, I was an observer, ever curious about what I was seeing that I didn't understand. As a child growing up in the postwar years, my family was in the retail business with what, by the 1950s, was a large store on 110th Street and Broadway in New York City. Wollman's department store was a wonderful business environment for a young child to explore. My grandmother was the matriarch of the business. A widow, she and her second husband, Abe, grew Wollman's over the years into a small retailer.

My parents expanded the size of the store in the 1950s and 1960s, increasing the scope of its merchandise so you could get most anything you needed from one store. They had men's and women's clothes, as well as clothing for children. Wollman's sold shoes and home goods and electronics and jewelry. It wasn't a Bloomingdale's or a Macy's; it was more of a miniature version of those on a square block in uptown Manhattan. Located outside of the subway stop and near Columbia University, the store served the neighborhood and served it well.

As I grew up, I spent Saturdays hanging shirts on hangers in the basement, with my grandmother observing us and correcting me as needed. There was only *one* way to hang a shirt at Wollman's, as I learned quite fast. I also watched my grandmother methodically count the daily receipts. Her record-keeping was completely manual, and her precision was quite remarkable to me.

When my mother and grandmother went into the market to buy merchandise for the store, I would often join them. As a young girl, I watched carefully, and they showed me what to look for. Somehow, I was absorbing their legacy, the years of buying merchandise and hoping for the best. Once I asked my grandmother how she knew what to buy, and she said, "Andrea, I really don't know. I know that whatever we buy for the store, about one-third will sell at full price, one-third will sell at a discount or sales price, and one-third will walk out the door." There might not have been any magic or data to support it, but watching them try and outsmart the odds was an art unto itself.

I watched myself going through my own evolution. If I was supposed to become a retailer, I never thought of myself as my mother or my grandmother. I was certainly not my father. He walked around all day with a serious face, deeply engaged in the business. So when I went off to college, I went wandering through classes as if I were on a discovery mission to find myself and what I was supposed to become. When I discovered anthropology, I had that epiphany when the brain goes "swish" and it all fits together. I had always been an observer and quite good at learning by listening and seeing. Anthropology offered an intellectual foundation to how we could better understand different societies and the cultures people created to survive in them. I was hooked.

I met my husband, Andy, in 1966 when I was nineteen and he was twenty-four. We met over the Fourth of July weekend at a camp on Schroon Lake where I was a counselor, and he was spending a week between jobs tending bar at his friend's lodge. While we sat on the beach, he asked me what I planned on being now that I was all grown up. I told him, in memorable lines, "Well, I am either going to be an attorney or an anthropologist." To which he responded, "Oh, be an anthropologist, and I will be here for you." Neither of us ever looked back. That was who I was, and he sort of knew it even then.

His support for me over the years took many forms, all of which were essential to my becoming who I thought I was. He supported my decision to go abroad to Greece to do my fieldwork. He helped me when I was doing my research in Astoria on Greek immigrants, and then when it came time to finish my dissertation, he lovingly pushed and prodded me to finish it. From the very beginning, he believed in me. I was never going to be just an ABD, "all but degree," if it was up to Andy.

As we raised two beautiful daughters, we shared roles, as I had a tenure-track professorial position at Ramapo College in New Jersey (now Ramapo University). Andy was a great teammate to help me pursue both motherhood and a career. I learned a great deal as a wife, an anthropologist, a professor, and a mother. In retrospect, it never seemed strange to be doing so many new things at once. As other professional or working mothers learn, there is no single priority. Everything is top priority. For me, I had to focus on my daughters first while never letting the rest suffer. The college was great. Then I took my daughters to Greece with me when they were four and five so I could study Greek women. My girls were part of the entire research. Little did they know about the adventure we were going on. Yet they learned to ride donkeys, enjoy a world without television, and find the only other English-speaking children on the island. They laughed, learned to swim, and accepted the experience—not that they had much choice. During this adventure, they taught me how special they were and how much fun it was to share my own passions with them.

Once I had my tenure, everything looked like a smooth journey ahead. That was until Andy became an executive at Citibank during the period when banking was being deregulated. Banking was going through a massive transformation. At a bank cocktail party, Andy introduced me to a number of senior executives. One conversation led to another, and someone asked if I could come over to Citibank to help them change. It didn't take long to see the creative opportunities happening there, from turning service people into sales mavens and tellers into ATMs. Before long I was a consultant helping the Bronx-Westchester region re-create the roles for their branch operations.

The folks I worked with told me to stay around and get my MBA on the job. How cool was that, particularly since they had no idea what an anthropologist did? I knew enough about business, from standing at my grandmother's knees, that I enjoyed banking, particularly as the industry was changing. That's when I knew I could apply my skills and add additional value to the banking industry by helping them run things in new ways. I could help them change the way people did their jobs and create new stories about how this would benefit their customers and shareholders.

I spent four years at Citibank, taking on the most affected branch and turning it around, helping to launch Direct Access, banking by personal computing, and other new introductions. Then I was recruited to become the senior vice president of Poughkeepsie Savings Bank. Poughkeepsie was an hour north of my home and an easy commute. It was still the Bank of FDR and had $100 million in passbooks. There were no ATMs or devoted tellers, and staff were searching for some understanding of what was happening to banking just two hours south of them in Manhattan.

While I was there to help change the savings bank and its story, I learned quickly how our own human brain changes as it watches others change. I kept being that observer. I would hang out on the branch floors and listen to the folks talk to long time customers. Everyone was a long time customer. They had their first penny saved there. Shifting them to new types of savings and helping them buy other services became the challenge.

When I think back to those days, I was fascinated as I observed people doing their jobs as they had for ages. They came to work from 9 a.m. to noon and from 1 to 3 p.m., and if they didn't steal, they had a job at the bank for life. Customers came in to see tellers and deposited money as they always had. Money market accounts were revolutionizing the traditional savings accounts, and even the old passbook was being eliminated. And as banks could expand across states, they were out hunting for other banks to expand their footprints and grow their lending.

Along the way, I learned what it was like to ask secretaries to give up their IBM Selectric typewriters and their Wite-Out. It was time to embrace a computer with a printer. I even bought them a Panasonic computer with an attached printer, which was innovative at the time.

In the market we launched new branches, added ATMs, and acquired banks in the Carolinas, well before we could manage them remotely. The CEO was already seeing the power of regionalization. We had a long way to go to be competent enough to do regional banking, and the internal systems for everything from loan origination to check processing were quite archaic.

After launching a successful marketing campaign, "P.S. We Love

You," I became progressively more bored as I watched the savings bank grow. I learned that I loved the innovation at the beginning of the change process. As I put people into place to run the new organization, I realized they were better suited for the operational maintenance. I liked turnarounds or start-ups or unfilled spaces and knew that my work aligned more with initiating change rather than managing it. So rather than staying on to help them maintain what they had started and were managing quite well on their own, I began to think what my next venture would be.

As I was helping to move Poughkeepsie forward, a friend of mine was president of a commercial bank in the area, First National Bank of Highland. He and I were on the board of the Hudson Valley Philharmonic. One day he asked if I would like to join him to turn his bank around. His challenge was that this small bank was a part of M&T Bank, yet it was located in the Hudson Valley. He had made an acquisition of bank branches from Chemical Bank in Rockland County. It seemed like an easy thing to do. However, I quickly discovered it was anything but.

I took him up on his offer and became executive vice president of First National Bank of Highland. This was an interesting part of my journey. I found loans on yellow pad paper in folders, and we weren't sure if they had been paid or not. The acquired Chemical Bank customers had not been integrated into the systems, so their checks were in suspense accounts. While the bank had overdraft protection, they also held bank statements of those overdrawn customers. Consequently, we had months of microfiche research to do to get customers their checks and statements that were sitting in bank filing cabinets. And the teller turnover was terrible.

The finance department was located on top of Billy's Burp and Slurp, and the files all smelled of french fries and beer. Lending was in such a small space that people had to stand to let someone get by. This was the perfect assignment for an anthropologist, who at the time, and even now, had few fears of the unknown and a strong willingness to tackle any challenge. And tackle we did. The bank president and I rolled up our sleeves and developed a new data-processing system. Soon after, we worked to expand our branches into new markets. There was a need for new lenders and systems to process the checks, and someone to run that as well. So we got the bank set up to merge into its parent, M&T Bank.

A great deal of problem-solving comes from listening and assuming nothing. When times are changing, it is hard for people to envision what could be better and how to make it so. During the merger we worked with the team, both new hires and old regulars, and helped them step back and take a fresh look at what we had to do to move the organization forward. What was so exciting was how they worked together. They had to. No single individual could steady the ship or push it forward on their own.

A while later, after I had left what was now M&T Bank, I got a call from a former Citibanker I knew. She was recruiting for Montefiore Medical Center in the Bronx. They had a new president who wanted a strong branding and marketing arm to tell the story of what he was doing to rebuild the hospital. I joined them for a few years, building up that department, and then went with a number of Montefiore executives to become the first lay management team at a Catholic hospital, St. Joseph's Regional Medical Center in Paterson, New Jersey.

Moving from a Bronx hospital with a lot of Jewish doctors to a different inner-city Catholic hospital that was serving the poor was fascinating. While they each delivered care, they did it in different ways. At Montefiore I had entrepreneurial doctors who screamed at me. This was during the launch of managed care services, and they didn't know how to build their practices. At St. Joseph's, the Sisters of Charity took care of the poor, regardless of whether they could pay. It didn't take long for me to realize they had limited their cash flow; they had many denials from insurers, and they had no way to capture revenue from the care they were delivering. People also had been trained to wait for the sisters to tell them what to do. While at St. Joseph's, I experienced the horror of 9/11; we answered the phones for hours with family members searching for their loved ones.

After my experience there, the time was right for me to launch my own business. I had always been an entrepreneur working inside other companies. I had learned a great deal about business, and in some ways, I had taught others a lot about how observation could help them see things through a fresh lens and make changes.

It was 2002. And as John Rosica so aptly stated, I am a corporate anthropologist who helps companies change. In that one sentence he captured the essence of who I was, what I did, and what benefits I and my firm could offer to help others get to where they wanted (or needed) to go. As I launched Simon Associates, customers came along remarkably fast. After a few lunches and referrals, I had Marcal Paper, Centenary College, Montefiore, and Atlantic Health System, and I was on my way.

Looking back, I have never been brought on board because I did anthropology. I was hired because these companies needed to change. Exactly how an anthropologist could help was unclear to them. I used it as my magic sauce. They didn't care what I did or how I was going to do it. They just needed a fresh pair of eyes to help them redirect their business. I didn't want to sell hope. But each of them, and most of our clients over the years, has been able to see their challenges through that fresh lens that we brought with us to help them reignite their growth.

Over the years I have expanded our services, added to our tool kit, and adapted to the fast-changing consultative services world. In 2006, I met Renée Mauborgne as she was promoting her book at the Harvard Club. I was telling her how much I liked her work and how anthropological it was. She then said, "You should be a Blue

Ocean Strategist." I asked what that was, and she said, "I have no idea; let's make it up." So we made it up. I became a practitioner and went through their training and have developed a part of my business around Blue Ocean Strategy, which is heavily focused on visual observation. This strategy perfectly fit into the needs of our clients, who typically come to us when they are stuck or stalled—"on the brink," prompting the title of my latest book.

Over the years, Andy has been a serial entrepreneur, having built several successful businesses. Before joining my firm, he sold his last one in 2017 to Educational Testing Services after building it to become the fifth largest in the K-12 summative assessment space. As partners we continue to speak widely and produce our podcast. Together, we work with clients to help them turn their observations into innovations.

From the Observation Deck

As you can see from my story, my background in anthropology was paramount in helping businesses see, feel, and think in new ways. The marriage of anthropology and business is, in fact, a perfect and often necessary union. We think we know what we are doing because of the way the brain sees the world. It is difficult to see things that do not fit into that perception of our reality. As Margaret Heffernan wrote in her book *Willful Blindness*, we are indeed willfully blind. The habits of daily living make it so efficient to reject things that are new or unfamiliar that we are unable to see what is really happening. My advice to those of you interested in using your background in anthropology to help other businesses is to find out what the target businesses need and to discover how you can help them. Think from the outside in to create a demand for your approach and skills. By offering them a new way of seeing and thinking, they will soon be chomping at the bit for your services and insights.

When I am working with my clients, I like to ask them what is happening all around that they cannot see. I often take them out to do some anthropology with me. They ask me what it means to do anthropology, so I make it easy; we hang out. Our job is to help them see what clients or prospective clients are doing differently. We also show them the gaps in the services offered, as well as the possibilities to open new markets through value innovation, not just incrementalism. But it is not easy. They have a lot of unlearning to do. They learned in their careers or their MBA programs, even in their high school years, how to focus on what they know and to do it better. What I do is help them think about what they are missing, what they need to see. For business leaders, I help open their minds to what they could bring to the world, or at least the business and the community that they are working in and living within.

I was always an observer, even at my grandmother's knee. I have no idea how I found anthropology in college, or Blue Ocean Strategy later on. They were as much serendipity as they were planned. For those of you still searching, I am certain that if you stay open to what could be, you will find your way. Your brain does a funny thing when it has an "aha" moment. It feels like a big "swish." You somehow know that this is right for you. You have to keep challenging and experiencing new things to know what is right. Humans need experiences to learn, which is why anthropology is so perfect for society and for businesses within that culture.

There are many women today cutting a path for you with their machetes. They feel like pioneers, blazing a trail in forbidden territories. I never felt like a pioneer, but I was. I always loved to see things change and to help others embrace the new with positive feelings and purpose. I hope those thousands of anthropologists who are in college can think about what they are studying, not from the perspective of themselves first but rather from the needs of others, be it business, not-for-profits, communities, government, the military, or wherever someone needs help to step out and see what is happening and how to make things better. Your future awaits. It is my hope that you enjoy your journey. As Margaret Mead said, "Anthropology demands the open-mindedness with which one must look and listen, record in astonishment and wonder that which one would not have been able to guess."

Rethinking the New Myths for Tomorrow

———————

"Women live longer than men. They do better in this
economy. More of 'em graduate from college. They go into
space and do everything men do, and sometimes they do
it a whole lot better. I mean, hell, get out of the way—these
females are going to leave us males in the dust."

—Ronald Ericsson, biologist

The Problem before Us

You may be asking how I chose these women and not others. In the course of writing *Rethink*, I conducted over fifty interviews and met many more women who could have easily been included. As I went over the stories, certain women's stories touched me in special ways. Since we decide through our feelings, my heart was driving my choices. Their stories were changing my way of seeing things. They do not, I admit, reflect the range of ethnic or religious sectors in our society, either in the US or globally. They also do not reflect all the industries, and many are missing, from Hollywood and music to politics and the military. Those are all important stories to share. They will come out in my podcasts and perhaps in my next book. Your story isn't in here either, and I bet you have either smashed a myth or are trying to right now. The book ends as it opens, searching for great stories to share that will help other women transform their lives and the society in which we are living. It is time to write our myths, our way.

As this book comes to a close, I want you to think about your own story and what your story reflects about our changing society and culture. What myths do you believe are holding you back from achieving what you want to do with your life? Are you going to be a myth-smasher too? If so, you will need to create a new story about how you overcame the glass ceilings, the brick walls, and the hurdles to achieve your own personal dreams.

This isn't a casual question and isn't only for women to answer. What happens to women affects their relationships with men, and these transformations are changing the way we work and live in America.

Ask yourself: Am I intentionally creating a life and crafting a story that will give me pleasure out of life, purpose every day, and a legacy that I want to leave to others? Are you watching as women all around you are transforming society by achieving goals that were unheard of not that long ago? In their wake, these women are leaving the men in the dust. This doesn't imply a career versus being a stay-at-home mom. It means thinking carefully about what matters to you and what your decisions will mean for others.

What's changing? Most everything. I asked at the beginning of this book if this movement wasn't more than the frustrations of women trying to become CEOs of major companies. Each of the stories showed how these women were pursuing their dreams in a changing world. Their advances and accomplishments were highlighting the way in which the entire culture was being changed. We discussed some major trends in each of the stories, and more are coming. As you read this, these trends are changing the context in which you and your friends are going to be living.

Some of the most important ones include: many women are living with men and not getting married. Some are not even bringing men into their homes or their lives. The running joke is that a guy is just another mouth to feed or one more PowerBar to share. And the women who do marry aren't getting married as early as they used to. Think about it: according to the US Census, in 1949, 78.8 percent of all households contained married couples. By 2009, sixty years later, 48.2 percent of households had married couples. The age of marriage had also increased. In 1956 the average age of marriage for men was twenty-two, and for women it was twenty. By 2019, the age at marriage was nearly thirty for men and twenty-eight for women.

Women have also become the major breadwinners, often earning more than their husband or partner. In one-third of the families in the US, women are the major breadwinners. By 2020, women make up more than 50 percent of the workforce. They have many of the skills that industry and companies need. I gave a speech to college presidents in Michigan not long ago, and one of the other speakers was from GM. He repeated a frequent appeal to the college presidents: he needed to hire ten-thousand employees, and could they please teach them to "communicate, coordinate, collaborate, create, and code." If they could do the first four, he would teach them to code. Who were the best at the first four? Women. And with the changes in manufacturing, construction, and industry and the advent of AI, machine learning, robots, bots, and IoT, the skills that are needed are not those of the past. The physical labor that men used to bring to the workplace is not in as great of demand. Now social skills, analytical skills, and collaborative skills are needed. And businesses are finding that women often come better able to insert their soft skills than their male counterparts.

Another trend is that almost 40 percent of the children in 2020 are now born to women who are not married. While this may reflect socioeconomic status differences, it also reflects the realization that men are not the income producers of the past. As David Brookes writes in his March 2020 issue of *The Atlantic*, the sacred idea of a nuclear family, born and raised in the 1950s and 1960s, may have been a mistake. What has emerged is a variety of family models, from a matriarchal one where grandmothers are helping mothers raise their children while also caring for their mothers, to young adults living at home with their parents or sharing living quarters among friends.

While working in Flint, Michigan, for four years as a consultant for a safety-net medical center, I was fascinated by the strength of the women caring for each other, in a metaphoric sisterhood. The African American community there was matriarchal, with the women caring for and managing each other carefully, enabling each of them to work, raise their children, and have fulfilling lives, often without a husband or male companion.

Multigenerational families are living together. One in four young adults aged twenty-five to thirty-four have moved into their parents' home (about 2.2 million) and do not go to school or work. On the other hand, many elders are moving into their children's homes as their need for better, more affordable housing and companionship counter the traditional model of isolated homes for single families.

When it comes to higher education, women are not only getting educated but are also using their education to enter the job market and build careers. What's more, for every two men who get a BA, three women will do the same. The men are entering college, beer-bashing, and dropping out, whereas women are outshining men in their studies and accomplishments. While they may not be entering the STEM programs to the degree that people would like them to, women are nevertheless expanding their reach into all walks of life.

Little holds women back from choosing a career in something that matters to them. They can go into law or medicine, research or business, or teaching and nursing. But they are also deciding to stop these ladder-climbing careers and stay at home to care for their children, or they turn to nonprofits to pursue employment that brings them better fulfillment. They bring their focus, creative problem-solving, and knowledge to everything they do. They don't have anything stopping them except the companies or industries, like the executive levels of Hollywood or aerospace, where they are still unwelcome or at least not recognized as talented, successful equals. What matters is less what they are not doing—like going into STEM—and more what they *are* doing (changing the place of women in society).

With 40 percent of the businesses in the US owned by women in 2019, this means women are employing over two million people. One in five firms with over a million or more in revenue is owned by a woman, and that is up 34 percent since 2018. Stephanie Breedlove and Celeste Ford are both trendsetters in this arena.

While not all women are succeeding, many are bundling a few small businesses to make a living outside of a corporate environment. Whether it is combining childcare with Uber driving or call center answering services with elder care, these women are trying to build a life with the flexibility they need to also run their families and even care for an unemployed spouse. And, as we emphasized in Delora's chapter, a large percentage of these are start-ups run by African American women who have run out of patience with the white male corporate workplace.

Finally, female executives, be they a CFO or a CEO, generate far better financial returns for their corporations than those firms led by men. Research by Quantamental Research from year-end 2002 to May 31, 2019, found that "public companies with women CEOs or CFOs often were more profitable and produced better stock price performance than many of the companies that had appointed men to those roles."

Men, as Hanna Rosin writes in her book *The End of Men: And the Rise of Women*, are struggling with these strong, educated, and capable women. And they are uncertain of their own roles in a society where physical labor is being upended by the need for smarts and creative abilities to manage in the new, emerging workplace—the one being created by the Fourth Industrial Revolution that Sam Rad is so readily tapping into.

What Do These Cultural Trends Mean for You?

You are a bright woman facing your own future. I'm sure you're wondering what these trends mean for you and for other women. Like many other women, you will need to figure out how your story will reflect how you are balancing conflicting values and searching for relationships with men and with women that offer meaning, friendship, and fun.

I'm reminded of Joseph Campbell, who wrote, "Myths are clues to the spiritual potentialities of the human life." Like the myths Campbell references, the stories of the women in this book were shared in part because they were all grounded in their spiritual potentialities. They each had a larger purpose, far beyond monetary success. Unlike men, these women are motivated by something bigger than simply a paycheck. They were telling us how their lives have purpose, how they have helped others, and how they are changing their industry or company. Their stories are forming a new mythology. By sharing their stories, they are also inviting you to help create the next generation of myths through your own story.

Rethinking your story is not easy. You are your story. It is your identity and has been since childhood. As John Holmes, the psychologist, wrote, "People think that the story creates their identity when in fact the story becomes their identity." Your story might have been created in a world that no longer exists. You might be in your fifties and searching for the next phase in your personal journey. Or you could be in high school and trying to imagine what you might do as you grow up. Like Evelyn Medvin, you might have a curiosity or a passion that is taking you someplace. You might not be sure what the new myth or story will become, but the time might be right for you to rethink your future story, create a new myth, and smash any that are holding you back. And if you are struggling, I encourage you to reach out for the invaluable support of friends and others in your community who can help you see what is possible and encourage you along the way.

Marian Wright Edelman said it so well: "You can't be what you can't see." She was so right.

As you think about your career and your personal life, consider how you want to visualize your future. It is important to see what is possible. We are learning much more about the power of visualization when creating future stories, as well as the roles they play in living our lives in the present. This means that our visualization of our future matters to how we live today. So it is important to start thinking about how you are going to see yourself tomorrow so you can begin to live a better life now.

The Power of Myth and the Role of Stories

When I first thought about writing this book, I knew I wanted to share the stories that these amazing women had told me about their journeys. Some of the women I had known a long time. Others I had just met. As I listened to each of their stories, I was struck by how they were changing me. My own story was being shifted around as I reflected on my own life and theirs. This is the power of story. It is the secret of our success.

It became important to share these stories with my grand-daughters and my grandson. Could they see different futures for themselves through the lens of these stories? These women were helping to change what women and men could achieve in their own lives. As I reflected on my own life, both of my daughters had grown up with a full-time professional mother, as my husband and I had both done. My daughters are now the third generation to become professional working moms and wives, with wonderful spouses who support them, just as my husband did. I often laugh about how Andy promised and was indeed always there for his anthropologist wife. He and I, and my daughters, each had role models. I am not sure our mothers were mentors. But our daughters could see how we navigated through tricky waters, building careers, adjusting to bad ones, and reemerging even stronger when we had to veer left or right as businesses thrived or cratered.

As I thought about these stories, I realized that each of these women had their own support system, be it spouses, family, partners, mentors, or others who had seen their personal vision and helped them achieve it. There was no one type of family or support network. They each had their own. Often it began in their childhood. But their stories never ended, as there are still parts yet to be written. These women were not soloists. They were part of a larger orchestra helping them to achieve their vision. Together they were creating the music and playing it at the same time. And there wasn't much of a model for them to follow. Instead, they were jumping out of metaphorical airplanes and building the parachute on the way down.

The exciting part of their stories and their storytelling was the mythical framework to it. The women did not realize it, but they were telling me their personal myths as they spoke. Some were slaying a dragon. Others were on a journey. As you are thinking about your own story, reflect on which type of mythology best reflects what you are attempting to achieve.

For example, are you slaying the dragon, like Delora Tyler in her aim of restoring balance to the world? Think about Delora's challenge as she had to overcome the men in those business meetings and establish herself as a strong, creative, competent woman. And she did. You can too.

Or perhaps your story is that of a rebirth. You could be threatened by a shadow that seems nearly victorious, until the sequence of miraculous events leads to redemption and rebirth and the restoration of a happier world. In many ways, this is Jamie Candee's story. Whether she was rebuilding Questar or Edmentum, she had a leadership style that engaged others to reach higher and achieve greater success, following her in ever challenging times.

Of course, there is also the myth grounded in the quest. You as the hero, often with sidekicks, travel in search of a priceless treasure and must defeat evil and overcome powerful odds. When you are on this type of quest, it ends when the heroine gets both the treasure and the prince. This is the story of every bold leader like Maria Gallo, who had to change Delaware Valley University and help it adapt to fast-changing times, using her treasures to get there. Or in some ways it is how Celeste Ford shined as she took all of her learning to create an amazing business where people love to come to work every day to make major advancements in aerospace and other industries.

Myths are also about people on their journey. These are stories of people who are suddenly thrust into strange and alien worlds and must make their way back to normal life once more. In some ways, both Babette Ballinger and Janine Firpo took their own journeys through their life, particularly when they went abroad, whether it was on $5 a day or on a bootstrap. They had to find their calling. And when they returned, they were reborn and ready to take on new careers with a heightened awareness of their own strengths. It was so interesting that each of them came back to a world that had changed.

Rags-to-riches myths appear in these women's stories as well. This type of myth occurs when a modest, downtrodden character achieves a happy ending when their natural talents are displayed to the world and they overcome their naysayers, or their competitors, with great success. This was clearly Evelyn Medvin and Stephanie Breedlove. They each took their own path to build something important for others. They didn't start with rags per se, but they did start from the ground up and were able to create richness for themselves and others as they followed their true path.

Tragic myths are often the result of humans overreaching. Their stories are all about how they have to get through a difficult time to emerge as heroes or heroines. Tragic stories deal with the big themes of love, loss, pride, the abuse of power, and the fraught relationships between men and gods. While I am not sure Andie Kramer or Sam Rad would think of their stories as tragedies, they have and probably will continue to have to push away men-controlled environments to achieve the greatness they have accomplished in the past. While they see no bounds, others do not necessarily welcome them in to help build new worlds.

I am not sure if my own story is one filled with irony. It might be seen as one where I was laughing all along the way as I watched others trying to adjust to changes without the skills or insights needed to embrace the new and discard the old. I don't think of it as a comedy or a tragedy. It was a journey, and it is one I am still on.

As you are reflecting on your own mythology, think about your story as you would share it today and what you would like it to be tomorrow. Oprah Winfrey credits her success to doing one thing over and over again while visualizing what she could be. She told interviewers after she was offered the part of Sofia in the movie *The Color Purple* that it was because of how she managed her brain. She literally believed, and we would agree, that she could find a way into that movie with tremendous focus, literally nonstop, with positivity and determination. And it is this law of attraction that is prevalent in each of the stories in this book and is included in your very own tool kit for you to explore in the Resources section of this book. So focus, focus, focus, and see what you can be.

The Road Ahead

In the 2016 US presidential election, Hillary Clinton was defeated in the Electoral College by Donald Trump. But she won the popular vote by several million. While she came close, she was unable to break the glass ceiling that has prevented women from becoming president in this country. While there may be a few chips in this ceiling, as evidenced by the six women who ran powerful campaigns in the 2020 primaries for the Democratic presidential candidate, none of them could outrun Joe Biden or Bernie Sanders. Each of the women was capable, articulate, and beautiful, with exceptional careers and demonstrated abilities. Yet the post-primary discussion was how the US was just not ready for a woman president. Unfortunately, this myth remains very powerful.

However, in Congress women are breaking through a ceiling that up until recently has been guarded heavily by men. The US House of Representatives was able to dramatically change its mix of men and women in the 2018 election with one hundred new women filling the 435 seats. Of these, forty-two are women of color, and at least three are LGBTQ. And twelve women won US Senate seats in the 2018 election, increasing the number of women senators to twenty-six of the hundred seats that exist. It was an exciting time to be a woman, even if it dramatically highlighted the challenges still before us.

Then there are those industries, from the executive levels of Hollywood to aerospace, where women are viewed as those barbarians at the gates. They are making inroads, albeit slowly and with reluctant men holding on tightly to the controls. It is hard to forget the 2020 Academy Awards, when female directors were shut out of the Best Director category again, even though women-directed movies were box office hits that year. Only five women have ever been nominated for Best Director in the ninety-two-year history of the awards, and only one, Kathryn Bigelow, ever won.

Today, women are rising up and pushing through, albeit not always as smoothly as they might wish. We are still struggling with a culture where women are viewed as less inspiring and less valuable than men. The road ahead for women in our country, and around the globe, comes from a world where men have, for millennia, crafted the rules, controlled the playing field, and defined what they would allow women to do. Ironically, there are fractures in those worlds. In part, they are coming from the growing realization that men and women are indeed different, but that doesn't make men better than women. The differences are there for a reason. They have different roles to play in our evolutionary vitality.

As a futurist, I am watching as our society is responding to the COVID-19 pandemic and to the Fourth Industrial Revolution. Each, on its own, is transformational. During the pandemic we are seeing a new world emerge. On the one hand, everyone is being asked (or forced) to work remotely, to stop attending events, to forget about going to in-person colleges, to eat at home, and to find something else to do instead of watching those music or sporting events in person. Most everything that was our habit in the past has been disrupted. There is nothing worse for people to be betwixt and between. We are happiest in our box, even if it is not a good one.

However, perhaps this disruption will result in an entirely new myth for our society about working remotely and the changes in our workforce and technology that are needed to support it. I often say if you want to change, have a crisis or create one. A crisis forces you to rethink what has always been so you can create new opportunities for your future. It is true that the story we create about our future is part of our ability to envision what is coming next. As we navigate these uncertain times, I invite you to use them to rethink your own story and to smash any myths that are holding you back from becoming the woman you want to become. If you have any new myths that you have smashed, I want to hear all about it.

Let's get started.

PART THREE

Tools to Use to Smash Myths and Create New Successes

The Smashing Myths Tool Kit

There is a path that comes from these stories that can create a tool kit for you to use. I bet you are ready to envision your own future and create the story about how you did it as you smash social myths and create new successes.

Since we have spent so much of our careers helping people and their organizations change, we thought we would put together some ideas that have a process behind them, building on the stories in the book, the research from the neurosciences and psychology, and the trends we see happening all around us.

Remember what Oprah preaches: what you believe is what you will see. Therefore, you need to imagine what you want to become, focus on how to make that possible, and stay focused on it.

It is time now to rethink your new story and begin to see it becoming true. If Martin Seligman is correct that we are *Homo Prospectus*, in his book by the same name, humans live in the moment because we are continuously envisioning the future. We are really futurists, worrying about what is coming and how to anticipate it. Envisioning the future is not that difficult. Your brain is doing it all the time. You just need to begin to focus on what you want tomorrow and make it happen.

Let's begin:

1. First, we have to have a visual awakening of who you are now. Tell a story about yourself as you are today. Being granular, draw a picture of yourself or create a list to show—

   a. Yourself—what you love and don't love; what you do and don't do
   b. Your life now and its joys and challenges
   c. Your interests—what you love to do and what you wish you didn't have to do
   d. Your dreams—your "if onlys . . ."

2. Get specific, and as literal as you can be. Put your list or drawing in a prominent place where you can see it for a while. It is a time to look in the mirror and see who you are now.

3. Next, it is time to visualize yourself in the future. This is a time to dream with a strong dose of reality to the dream. Visualization is what will help you transform the person you are now into the one you would like to become. Think about what will make you—

   a. Become who you believe you can be
   b. Know what would make you happy
   c. Realize how you might be personally fulfilled
   d. Understand how you can be professionally accomplished
   e. Build a happy family
   f. Enjoy the support of your friends and community
   g. Know what matters to you and how you want your story to develop

4. If you were writing your story in five years or when you have achieved your desired goals, what would your new story be? Write it out or draw a picture, maybe even several.

5. Once you have your future vision storied out, begin to think about how you might get there. Here is where you start to wonder and live your life, reflecting on how today is going to move you forward toward the you of tomorrow. What might this mean? To help you get started, here are some suggestions:

   a. Create some milestones that are small wins for you to achieve if you are going to become the vision you have for yourself. Literally put your milestones down on a piece of paper with dates and timelines. By this date, I will have _____, because it is the next (first) step toward becoming who I want to be. Stories change with small wins that build your confidence.

   b. What would you eliminate, reduce, raise, or create to build a new you? Be honest with yourself and make a chart with some action items.

   c. Put some dates on your action items. Think about the women in this book and their stories. Some were more focused than others. Some were sure of what they wanted to achieve but not sure how to get there. Others were living out their life, while others were helping them see their potential. There was no single path. But they each had their journey and were moving forward to reach some goal along the way. Maria Gallo might not have aspired to be a college president, for example, but others saw her potential. And Andie Kramer knew she wanted to be an attorney, and nothing, not even that person who told her not to become an attorney, stopped her.

   d. Get clear on your dream, your life path, and how you will see your steps as part of something bigger.

   e. Celebrate, often. Whether you are an entrepreneur trying to build a big business or a great leader seeking the right place to move forward, you need to pause often and take stock of your progress and celebrate. Humans need to celebrate. It lets the prize seem even better.

6. Keep a diary. There is exceptional research that shows us that people who keep diaries achieve their goals and do so with extraordinary results, far better than those who don't keep diaries. That might seem strange, but it is easy enough to try. Online or on paper, keep your story coming, write it, and reread it. Let it help you believe. Embrace your new focus and belief that "yes, you can."

7. Stop your brain from undermining you. Every time you say, "No, that won't work," convert it to a "Yes, that's a great idea." You can manage negative thoughts by simply thinking that you can.

8. Build up your idea bank. The research is compelling. The more ideas you have, the more likely you will have big ones. They come at the intersections of all the ideas you entertain. Keep a little idea book, and keep those ideas coming. Try to stay focused on the vision you have for yourself as you build your idea bank.

You are writing a new story. Don't let your brain delete great ideas because they don't fit into your current story. Keep saying, "Yes, that's a great idea." Pretty soon, you will achieve the goals that you aspire to all through your life's journey.

Questions to Discuss

1. This is a book to help you "see what you can be." How do you feel as you read these women's stories?

2. To which of the stories could you most relate? Which of the myths has affected you?

3. What hurdles have you faced in your own journey? How have you been able to overcome them?

4. For each of these women, their growing-up years framed their lives. I remember standing at my grandmother's proverbial knees. When you think about your growing-up period in your life, what memories are the most vivid and seem to help you frame your own life story? What are your most poignant memories?

5. Several women spoke of their journeys away from their jobs and the discoveries they made about themselves. Have you taken time to discover yourself through a journey? Real and metaphoric journeys play important roles in framing our lives. Are you ready for yours?

6. How has each of these women reframed the world in which she was living to allow her to succeed when others thought she couldn't?

7. How have you thought about reframing your world to achieve your dreams? Is it time? Or is your story a perfect one for you?

8. Have you always wanted to be an entrepreneur like Stephanie Breedlove? She saw an unmet need and turned it into a successful business. What unmet needs have you seen that could be your big business opportunity?

9. Women are said to have far better social skills than men, but when they use those skills, they don't always achieve the respect of men. Jamie Candee was an exceptional leader because she knew how to use her skills to get men and women to embrace her vision and follow her. How can women change the power structure and use their leadership to greater societal benefit?

10. Babette Ballinger had a life journey that required her to help men succeed. They grew in great part because of her talent. Then she turned her skills into a successful business for herself. I love her story because she never stopped believing in herself. What are your thoughts about her life's challenges and your own?

11. Andie Kramer has been smashing the myths holding back female attorneys ever since she was a child and wanted to become a lawyer. Now she is helping other women do the same by educating them. How could you turn your experiences into hope to help other women?

12. Janine Firpo is proud of how her mother showed her how to become a successful businesswoman. Now she wants to help other women think about money more wisely and manage and invest it successfully. For you, who is your financial role model? How can you best learn from them? How do you view your earnings and your savings? How do you manage "risk"?

13. Perhaps you have been thinking about how you can help turn around colleges and universities in today's troubling times. Each institution is unique but the same. They need some new innovative thinking about how to offer promise and purpose to a wider audience. Is this something you can help achieve? They are waiting for strong women leaders like Maria Gallo to help them see a way forward that is agile and adaptive to fast-changing times. Give thought to how Maria's story could be your own.

14. Delora Tyler, like so many of us, couldn't stand the dynamics of the workplace where the men ignored what she had to say. Instead, she created a successful business where men embraced her talent and her wisdom. Have you had to cope with situations where you and your ideas were ignored? How did you get your ideas heard and acted upon? How can you change your own conversational style to ensure that women and men are listened to, ideas are heard, and respect is shown?

15. Evelyn Melvin became the woman she always wanted to be and was able to turn her love for geology into a successful career. Are you interested in something that could become your own career? Are you finding a way to live that dream?

16. Celeste Ford told us her story to encourage women to find a path into aerospace at a time when they are needed. Was she unique, or could other women follow in her footsteps? Why did women fall out of the aerospace world even after they led it during the development of the airplane? How can women see this as an opportunity and capitalize on it?

17. Sam Radocchia is telling you her story even as a *Forbes* 30 Under 30. She has miles to travel, yet she has already built a life filled with success and pleasure. Whether it was skydiving or creating a new blockchain business, Sam sees what she wants to do and then gets it going. But she is not one to stay around until it matures. It is in the early adventure that she finds her best experiences. What about you? What is holding you back, or how are you moving forward? It isn't easy, as Sam will tell you. She is now looking for the next adventure, and they aren't always in plain sight.

18. I shared my story because I want anthropologists to have opportunities in business and society well beyond what is available

today. Are you in the social sciences, and have you found your path forward too? How can we help others create the opportunities that their training and perspective offer to help solve problems in new ways? Isn't it time for all of us to see the future through a fresh lens—and how can you be part of that transformation as well?

19. Each of these women is telling you her story for a reason. Think of them as gifts to you and to other women. They are role models—or could be. Think about your own story. Have these women helped you rethink your own story? Would you tell it in the same way tomorrow as you might have told it yesterday? Now is the time to ask: How can I smash the myths that are keeping women from achieving the success they deserve, now and in the future?

20. In each of the stories I have gently included some insights into the role of a partner, spouse, or significant other in the lives of these women. What are your thoughts about the ways in which a teammate could help you be the woman you aspire to become? I dedicated the book to these women and to my husband, Andy, because I could not have been "me" without "we."

Organizations

American Business Women's Association
(https://bit.ly/3bmNLXk)

Black Women Business Owners of America
(https://bit.ly/2WM7uM0)

The Female Entrepreneur Association
(https://bit.ly/39hGozb)

Goldman Sachs 10,000 Small Businesses program
(https://bit.ly/3btPYjT)

Ladies America
(https://bit.ly/39oY8Zk)

Ladies Who Launch
(https://bit.ly/2UIa1nM)

National Association for Female Executives
(https://bit.ly/2vUpn0g)

National Association for Women Business Owners
(https://bit.ly/2UiMKtQ)

National Association of Women Lawyers
(https://bit.ly/33Pr0bS)

Sally Ride Science
(https://bit.ly/2JeP8ez)

Women's Business Enterprise National Council
(https://bit.ly/33RTYrJ)

Women's Business Exchange
(https://bit.ly/2vUpb12)

Resources to Help
You Rethink Your Story

Amott, Teresa and Julie Matthaei. *Race, Gender, and Work: A Multicultural Economic History of Women in the United States.* Boston: South End Press, 1996.

Breedlove, Stephanie. *All In: How Women Entrepreneurs Can Think Bigger, Build Sustainable Businesses, and Change the World.* Austin, TX: Greenleaf Book Group, 2017.

Campbell, Joseph. *The Hero with a Thousand Faces.* New York: Pantheon Books, 1949.

Cohen, Allan R. and David L. Bradford. *Influence Without Authority*, 3rd edition. Hoboken, NJ: Wiley, 2017.

Cuddy, Amy. *Presence: Bringing Your Boldest Self to Your Biggest Challenges.* Boston: Little, Brown, 2015.

Duckworth, Angela Lee. *Grit: The Power of Passion and Perseverance.* New York: Scribner, 2016.

Dweck, Carol. *Mindset: How You Can Fulfill Your Potential.* New York: Ballantine Books, 2016.

Grenny, Joseph, Kerry Patterson, David Maxfield, Ron McMillan, and Al Switzler. *Influencer: The New Science of Leading Change*, 2nd edition. New York: McGraw-Hill, 2013.

Kramer, Andrea S. "Recognizing Workplace Challenges Faced by Black Women Leaders." *Forbes* (January 7, 2020).

Kramer, Andrea S. and Alton B. Harris. "Are Your Work Friendships Only with People Who Look Like You?" *Harvard Business Review* (September 9, 2019).

Kramer, Andrea S. and Alton B. Harris. "The Goldilocks Dilemma: Why Career Advancement Is So Much Harder for Women Than Men and What Women Can Do to Change That." Change This. May 4, 2016. https://andieandal.com/goldilocks-dilemma.

Kramer, Andrea S. and Alton B. Harris. *It's Not You, It's The Workplace: Women's Conflict at Work and the Bias That Built It.* London: Nicholas Brealey, 2019.

Kramer, Andrea S. and Alton B. Harris. "Overcoming Women's Workplace Conflicts Because of Different Social Identities." Change This. September 4, 2019. https://www.porchlightbooks.com/blog/ changethis/2019/overcoming-womens-workplace-conflicts -because-of-different-social-identities.

Kramer, Andrea S. and Alton B. Harris. "Taking Control: Women, Gender Stereotypes and Impression Management." *Women's Bar Association of Illinois Newsletter* (Winter 2014).

Lévi-Strauss, Claude. *Myth and Meaning: Cracking the Code of Culture.* Toronto: University of Toronto Press, 1978.

Lévi-Strauss, Claude. *Mythologiques (Introduction to a Science of Mythology): 4 volumes,* translated by John Weightman and Doreen Weightman, 1969–1982. Chicago: University of Chicago Press, 1983.

Leyba, Cara Alwill. *Girl Code: Unlocking the Secrets to Success, Sanity, and Happiness for the Female Entrepreneur.* New York: Passionista Publishing, 2015.

Patterson, Kerry, J. Grenny, R. McMillan, and A. Switzler. *Crucial Conversations: Tools for Talking When Stakes Are High,* 2nd edition. New York: McGraw-Hill, 2011.

Perez, Caroline Criado. *Invisible Women: Data Bias in a World Designed for Men.* New York: Abrams Press, 2019.

Pinker, Susan. *The Sexual Paradox: Men, Women, and the Real Gender Gap*. New York: Scribner, 2008.

Rosin, Hanna. *The End of Men and the Rise of Women*. New York: Riverhead Books, 2012.

Shook, Ellyn and Julie Sweet. *When She Rises, We All Rise, Getting to Equal 2018: Creating a Culture Where Everyone Thrives*. Accenture, 2018.

Simon, Andi. *On the Brink: A Fresh Lens to Take Your Business to New Heights*. Austin, TX: Greenleaf Book Group, 2016.

Sincero, Jen. *You Are a Badass: How to Stop Doubting Your Greatness and Start Living an Awesome Life*. Philadelphia: Running Press Book Publishers, 2013.

Wheeler, Tarah. *Women in Tech: Take Your Career to the Next Level with Practical Advice and Inspiring Stories*. Seattle, WA: Sasquatch Books, 2016.

Some Additional Tools for You

I encourage each of you to become anthropologists in your own right by cultivating an ongoing sense of curiosity about your world and your relationships.

As you begin to craft your own story to smash those myths that have been holding you back, please reach out and share your journey with us at info@andisimon.com. We are happy to help you share it with others and wish you all the best with your new successes.

Acknowledgments

Writing a book is both humbling and inspiring. When my husband, Andy, and I launched the Simon Initiative at Washington University in St. Louis to help women entrepreneurs, we were struck by the recurring things women were asking of us: "Show me the way." They were looking for role models, others who had done what they were trying to do, as well as methods and lessons learned to bring some certainty to the uncertainty they were facing. I began to write this book to help find role models for these aspiring women. They needed the stories from other women. Then as I was working on the book, Andy and I were driving to Nantucket, and I was telling him about the stories and how they were changing me and my own story. That's when he said, in his brilliant way, "These women are 'smashing the myths' of women in business." Just like that, the book had a new purpose and a new title. Andy, thank you. This book is from you to all these women searching for themselves as you helped me find myself.

Then it was time to rewrite the interviews. Each woman had a different story to share. And once I started, I wanted to talk to even more women, to learn how they smashed their own myths. They each were generous, abundantly so, with their time and their insights. I want to express my deepest gratitude to each of these ten women who allowed us to tell their stories. And I want to thank the forty others whom I could not include in this book. Perhaps there will be a next one for you.

For each of these women, I hope I have done your life's story the service it deserves. You were so kind to work carefully with me as we crafted your story. Your journey reflects your personal desire to help other women, and men, rethink their own lives. We didn't want the world, as Simone de Beauvoir wrote in 1949, to be the work of men alone, as it has been for millennia. As we say so often, the only truth is that there is no truth. And it was time for all of us to start to change the story, smash the myths, and write the new ones that will change the world. Thanks to each of you for helping us bring forth your stories that will help change this world for the better.

Diana Ceres, my amazing editor, I hope the impact of the book can say "thank you" far more than my own heartfelt thank-you can on its own. I don't think anyone who has not written a book understands the role of the editor in helping the author take good ideas and make them come alive on each page and in its entirety. Diana, you were my mentor and my inspiration. Thank you.

I was writing this book for my amazing daughters, Alexandra and Rachel, and my grandchildren, Michael, Katharine, and Lulu, and my very special sons-in-law, Aaron and John. We live our lives for our children and their children. We dream their dreams with them and hope we have helped them achieve them. Thank you for being such a great joy and for being so patient with me. I am endlessly proud of you.

Greenleaf Book Group—you are the best publisher for me. Our styles work so well together, and the trust I have in your judgment cannot be easily expressed. You bring out the best in all of your authors, particularly in this one.

I have to end with a thank-you to my parents, from wherever they might be watching. Growing up was, on reflection, an important part of becoming who I was then. Reading each of these stories, we know that growing up is helping us sort through who we are before we even know it.

Finally, thank you to my grandmother Miriam, who let me learn about life while standing at her knee.

Index

A

D

Davies, Auerbach, and Cornell law
   firm, 77
defense careers, 143. *See also* aerospace careers
Delaware Valley University (DelVal),
   113–114, 116–117, 121–123
Denny, Rita, 193–194
Department of Defense (DOD), 147
Detroit Institute of Arts (DIA), 165,
   166
Detroit News, 155–156, 163–165
diary, keeping, 224
Dinesen, Isak (Karen Blixen), 13
discrimination. *See also* myths about
   women in business
   communication to overcome, 85
   in STEM workplaces, 174
   against women in law firms, 79
diversity, value of, 89
doctors, black women, 159
*Doing Anthropology in Consumer
   Research* (Denny and Sunderland), 194
dragons, myths about slaying, 214
dream jobs, Stellar Solutions focus
   on, 149
Dubinsky, Donna, 176
Dutch colonists, 29–30

E

Eagly, Alice H., 8
Earhart, Amelia, 45
earth sciences. *See* geoscience careers
Easley, Anne, 175
Eckert-Mauchly Computer Corp.,
   175
Edelman, Marian Wright, 213
Edmentum, 51, 52, 214
education, cultural trends related to,
   210. *See also* higher education

Elsesser, Kim, 7–8
emerging markets, 101–103
employees
   company culture, 39–40
   Stellar Solutions' focus on, 149,
      151
   successful leadership, 51, 53
The End of Men (Rosin), 211
engineering careers, 173. *See also*
   aerospace careers
ENIAC computer, 174–175
entrepreneurs. *See also* specific entrepreneurs by name
   African American women as
      anthropological observations,
         168–170
      Delora Tyler, 161–168
      myth related to, 157–161
      overview, 155–157
   anthropological observations,
      37–41
   cultural trends, 211
   myth related to, 28–32
   overview, 27–28
   Stephanie Breedlove, 32–37
Equal Credit Opportunity Act, 94
Ericsson, Ronald, 207
Estée Lauder Company, 31
ethnographic research. *See*
   anthropology
Evans, Patty Davis, 67
evolution
   and psychology of gender, 19–22
   role of stories and myths in, 14
executives, female, 211. *See also* leadership roles
Experience 360 program (DelVal),
   123
experiential learning, 123
expertise, value of, 137
Explorer Post program (Citgo), 130

About the Author

Andrea J. Simon, PhD, Corporate Anthropologist, President of Simon Associates Management Consultants

Andrea J. Simon, PhD, ("Andi") is an international leader in the growing field of corporate anthropology, an award-winning author, and founder and CEO of Simon Associates Management Consultants (SAMC). SAMC was founded two decades ago to apply the theory, methods, and tools of anthropology to help companies, organizations, and communities adapt to changing times.

Her book *On the Brink: A Fresh Lens to Take Your Business to New Heights* won an Axiom Bronze Best Book award in 2017. *On the Brink* delves into the application of corporate anthropology to business problems. The seven case studies illustrate how anthropological methods can help companies see themselves in new ways—and reignite their growth strategies. Several of the companies were in need of a Blue Ocean Strategy, an area of Dr. Simon's expertise.

Before opening her consulting business in 2002, Dr. Simon held executive management positions in financial services and healthcare organizations, each of which was going through rapid change. She was a consultant at Citibank during the period of deregulation, as well as executive vice president of First National Bank of Highland and senior vice president of Poughkeepsie Savings Bank, all of which had to adapt to a new business landscape.

In the healthcare sector, she was the director of branding and marketing for Montefiore Medical Center and vice president for branding, marketing, and physician services for St. Joseph's Regional Medical Center.

Dr. Simon also was a tenured professor of anthropology and American studies at Ramapo College of New Jersey. In 2006, she was a visiting professor teaching entrepreneurship at Washington University in St. Louis. And in 2018, she and her husband and partner, Andrew Simon, launched the Simon Initiative in Entrepreneurship at the Skandalaris Center at Washington University in St. Louis.

A trained practitioner in Blue Ocean Strategy, Dr. Simon has conducted over four hundred workshops and keynote speeches between 2007 and 2020. She also has worked with a wide range of clients to help them find their own Blue Ocean Strategies and is widely published on the topic.

A highly experienced consultant working on culture change, Dr. Simon uses the Organizational Culture Assessment Instrument (OCAI) developed by Dr. Kim Cameron and Dr. Robert E. Quinn. Dr. Simon is part of the consulting team licensed to use the OCAI-online in the Netherlands.

Dr. Simon is also a trained facilitator of Innovation Games®. SAMC uses Innovation Games widely as part of their approach to helping organizations see things with fresh eyes. SAMC's clients span the gamut of industries, from manufacturers to service companies to colleges and universities and innovative companies.

A contributor to *Huffington Post*, *Fierce Health*, and *Forbes*, Dr. Simon has been on *Good Morning America* and *ABC New York*. She has been interviewed in the *Washington Post* and published in *Business Week*, *American Banker*, *Daily News*, *INC Magazine*, the *Los Angeles Times*, *John Wiley Global Business*, and *Organizational Excellence*, among others.

Her podcast *On the Brink with Andi Simon* is ranked among the top two-hundred in business podcasts and the top twenty futurist podcasts, with over 3.2 million downloads. Her podcast brings together thought leaders, CEOs, entrepreneurs, authors, and business leaders to help people see, feel, and think about themselves and their businesses through a fresh lens.

Andi and her husband have two wonderful daughters, three amazing grandchildren, and two marvelous sons-in-law. Together they enjoy the gifts and challenges of their extraordinary lives.